SMALL CATS

Zefa-BAUER

Great Creatures of the World

SMALL CATS

Facts On File

Written by Susan Lumpkin

Facts On File, Inc.
460 Park Avenue South
New York NY 10016

Copyright © 1993 Weldon Owen Pty Limited
Copyright © 1993 Weldon Owen Inc.

Produced by Weldon Owen Pty Limited
43 Victoria Street, McMahons Point,
NSW 2060, Australia
Telex AA23038, Fax (02)929 8352
A member of the Weldon International
Group of Companies
Sydney • London • San Francisco

Chairman: Kevin Weldon
President: John Owen
General Manager: Stuart Laurence
Publisher: Sheena Coupe
Project Coordinator: Tracy Tucker
Copy Editor: Beverley Barnes
Assistant Editor: Veronica Hilton
Designer: Diane Quick
Main Illustrations: Frank Knight
Other Illustrations: Tony Pyrzakowski
Production Director: Mick Bagnato
Production Coordinator: Simone Perryman

Printed by Kyodo Printing Co. (Singapore) Pty Ltd
Printed in Singapore

A WELDON OWEN PRODUCTION

10 9 8 7 6 5 4 3 2 1

About the author

Dr. Susan Lumpkin received her Ph.D. in biological psychology, specializing in animal behavior, at Duke University. She was awarded a Smithsonian Institution Post-doctoral Fellowship for advanced study in mammalian behavior at the National Zoological Park. Dr. Lumpkin has conducted extensive research in mammalian and avian reproductive behavior and has written widely on animal behavior and conservation for general audiences. She was coordinating editor of *Wild Mammals in Captivity: A Guide to Management*, co-consulting editor on *Great Cats*, and is editor of the Friends of the National Zoo *Zoogoer* magazine.

Facts On File books are available at special discounts when purchased in bulk quantities for businesses, associations, institutions or sales promotions. Please call our Special Sales Department in New York at 212/683-2244 (dial 800/322-8755 except in NY, AK or HI).

Library of Congress
Cataloging-in-Publication Data:

Lumpkin, Susan
    Small cats / [written by Susan Lumpkin].
    p. cm. — (Great creatures of the world)
Includes index.
Summary: Describes the physical characteristics and behavior of the smaller feline species in their habitats around the world.
ISBN 0-8160-2848-6
1. Felidae—Juvenile literature [1. Felidae. 2. Cats.]
I. Title. II. Series
QL 737.C23L87 1993   92-26837
599.74'428—dc20   CIP AC

The author would like to acknowledge the following people whose contributions to *Great Cats* were drawn upon for this book:

Dr. Urs Breitenmoser
Dr. Louise H. Emmons
Dr. Gillian Kerby
Dr. Richard A. Kiltie
Dr. David W. Macdonald
Mr. Jeffrey A. McNeely
Dr. Jill D. Mellen
Dr. S. Douglas Miller
Mr. Warner C. Passanisi
Dr. Gustav Peters
Dr. James A. Serpell
Ms. Fiona C. Sunquist
Dr. Mel Sunquist
Dr. Ronald L. Tilson

Page 1: Not all cats hate water. Like this African wildcat, many cats go into water to cool off, and some even hunt in water.
Pages 2–3: A North American lynx and her cub explore a stream in Montana.
This page (top to bottom):
The black-footed cat is one of the smallest cats in the world.
The leopard cat thrives in a variety of habitats, from tropical forests to pine forests.
The wildcats of Europe, Asia, and Africa look like larger versions of the domestic tabby.
Opposite page: The plain-coated African caracal lives in dry wooded habitats, hunting birds, rodents, and small antelope.
Page 6: The Eurasian lynx is one of the largest of the small cats.
Page 7: (top) The kodkod is a rare cat that lives only in a small area of Chile and Argentina.
(bottom) The long-legged caracal is the heaviest of the small African cats.

Contents

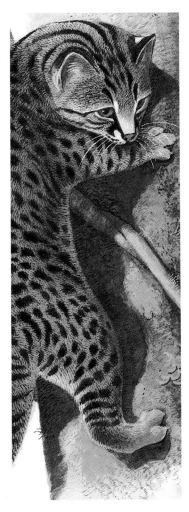

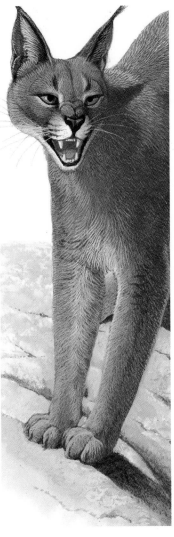

The small cats

The big cats are among the world's best-known animals. Almost everyone recognizes these magnificent predators: lions, tigers, jaguars, leopards, snow leopards, cheetahs, and pumas (cougars or mountain lions). But the rest of the world's cats, the little ones, are among the least known of the mammals.

Thirty different species

You have probably heard of bobcats and lynxes, but how about the kodkod, margay, and oncilla? There are 30 species (types) of small cats, all averaging less than about 66 pounds (30 kilograms) in weight. In contrast, the big cats can weigh in at more than 88 pounds (40 kilograms). This book will reveal what is known about the world of small cats—and also show how mysterious most of them remain.

The cat family

With their larger relatives, the small cats are members of the family Felidae. The cat family is one of seven families in a group of mammals called the order Carnivora. This order of mammals includes dogs, bears, seals and sea lions, hyenas, and other species with features designed for feeding on animal flesh. Mammals are animals that have fur or hair and feed their young on milk from mammary glands.

Of all the families in the order Carnivora (which means "meat eater"), the cats are most specialized for hunting and eating animals with a backbone. Unlike bears, for example, which mix a diet of meat with other items such as fruit and nuts, cats almost never eat anything but meat.

All the cats, both big and small, are remarkably alike in their general appearance and behavior, but each species has unique features that set it apart from the others.

Where are they found?

Small cats live in many different habitats, or environments, all around the world. Some species live in forests—tropical rain forests or northern evergreen forests—others in deserts or in grasslands. Some species hunt in trees, others hunt on the ground. One species, the fishing cat, hunts in rivers for fish. Others eat mice, birds, rabbits, and even small monkeys. The largest of the small cats, such as the clouded leopard and the caracal, prey on small antelope, deer, and goats.

▲ *The clouded leopard.*

How are they related?

"Big" and "small" are not important when scientists look at the whole family, even though size does make a difference in how the cats live and hunt. Scientists classify animals according to the similarities and differences in their skeletons and the rest of their bodies, but not all scientists agree on the same classification system. Most agree that the marbled cat, the clouded leopard, and five species of lynxes are more closely related to the big cats than to the other small cats. That is why they are classified in the subfamily Pantherinae with the big cats, while the rest of the small cats are put in the subfamily Felinae.

But new studies of the genetics of cats are changing this view. These studies divide the cats into three groups, or lineages (pronounced lin-ee-ages). One lineage, called the "ocelot lineage," includes seven species of small cats from South America. Another lineage, called the "domestic cat lineage," is made up of the wild ancestors of domestic cats and five other species of small cats from Asia and Africa. The rest of the small cats belong in the "Panthera lineage" along with the big cats.

Whatever their relationships, all of the cats, big and small, face an uncertain future in the wild. People around the world are working to save big cats from extinction, but at the same time, very few efforts are being made to save most of the rare and endangered small cats. It would be a shame if any of these mysterious cats were to become extinct before we had a chance to learn more about them.

Did you know?

Except for the polar regions and some islands, such as Madagascar, New Zealand, and Australia, nearly every place on Earth is home to at least one wild species of cat. And even islands that didn't have wild cats are now home to domestic cats, which people have taken to the farthest lands on the globe.

▲ *This wildcat kitten will become a powerful hunter.*

Jany Sauvanet/NHPA

Smallest of the small

The rusty-spotted cat of India and Sri Lanka is the world's smallest cat. With an average weight of 2¼ pounds (1 kilogram), it is about half the size of a typical domestic cat. Rusty-spotted cats are good climbers so they may hunt in trees for birds, small mammals, insects, reptiles, and frogs. They are rarely seen, so they probably live alone, hunt at night, and spend the day resting, hidden among the plants. Nothing more is known about them in the wild.

Ron Austing

The body of a cat

A cat has a perfect body for its life as a predator. Any differences between small cats and big cats—differences in the skeleton and other parts of the body—are almost entirely differences in size.

▼ *The skeletons of all cats are quite similar, although they vary in size.*

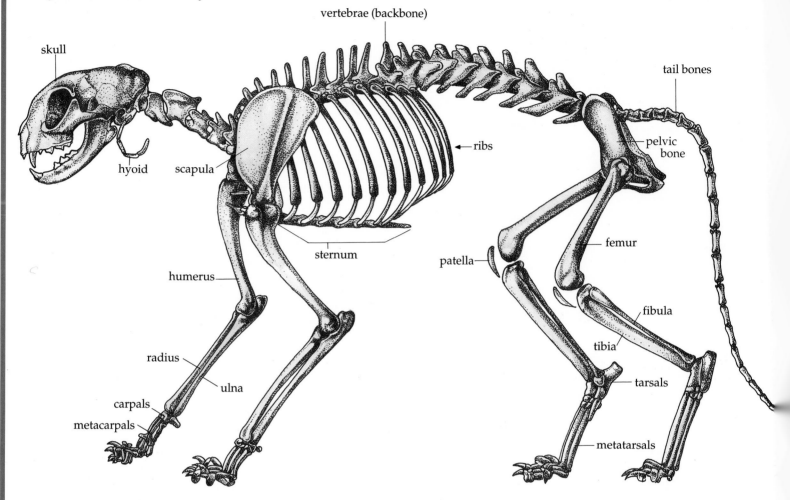

vertebrae (backbone)

skull

tail bones

ribs

pelvic bone

hyoid   scapula

femur

sternum

patella

humerus

fibula

tibia

radius

ulna

tarsals

carpals

metacarpals

metatarsals

The head

Let's start with the skull. A cat's skull has short, powerful jaws, with attachments for large jaw muscles, needed to kill and eat the animals it preys on. Most cats have 30 teeth (lynxes, golden cats, and caracals have 28), which are specialized for different purposes. Long canines are used for the bite that kills the prey. Bladelike premolars on the upper jaw and molars on the lower jaw are designed for shearing meat off bones.

The skull also gives us information about the cat's senses. Large eye sockets, placed toward the front, suggest that a cat has good vision and hunts by sight. Large eyes gather more light, which improves the cat's vision at night. The placement of the eyes gives the cat binocular vision—the ability to focus both eyes on a single object—which is necessary if a cat is to pounce accurately on its prey.

Cats have excellent hearing, far better than ours at high frequencies, which they use to detect their prey. Small cats can actually hear the sounds made at very high frequencies by rodents to communicate with each other.

Cats use the sense of smell mainly to detect other cats, and their sense of smell is far less acute than a dog's is. But it is helped by a structure in the mouth called the vomeronasal organ. Most cats exhibit a lip-curling grimace, called flehmen, which is usually seen when they sniff another cat. When they open the mouth like this, it allows the odor to reach the vomeronasal organ, and the information then proceeds to the brain.

Cats have a sensitive sense of touch, which is displayed in the way they use their whiskers. A cat's whiskers fan out in front of the mouth when the cat captures prey. Using whiskers helps the cat to judge where to place the killing bite.

The rest of the body

Most of the skeleton is designed for speed and power. Cats have long legs, and they even walk on their toes (in "digitigrade" locomotion) to make themselves taller.

▶ *Like all cats, the wildcat has excellent vision. Many people believe that cats are color-blind, but they are probably not. However, because they hunt mostly at night, when all colors fade to gray, cats are unlikely to pay attention to colors—they just aren't relevant.*

▲ *The serval has the largest external ears of any cat. It lives in the grasslands of Africa and depends on its sense of hearing to find its prey (mice, rats, etc.) in the tall grass. All cats have large external ears that turn to help them detect sounds.*

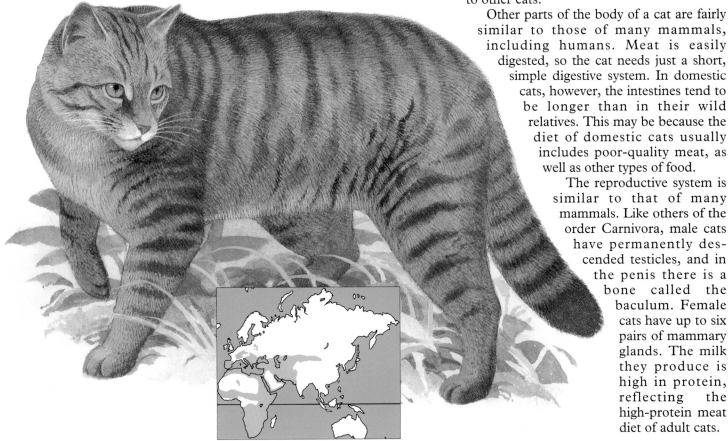

Their spine is very flexible, so cats can flex and arch their back to increase speed. This also enables a cat to twist and turn easily—the reason why a falling cat usually lands on its feet. Overall, the cat's body is fairly elastic, allowing it to move smoothly, and is slender, so that it can move easily through thick vegetation such as long grass and dense bushes. A long, flexible tail acts like a rudder to improve balance. You may have noticed that a cat's tail movements are very expressive, signaling its mood and intentions to other cats.

Other parts of the body of a cat are fairly similar to those of many mammals, including humans. Meat is easily digested, so the cat needs just a short, simple digestive system. In domestic cats, however, the intestines tend to be longer than in their wild relatives. This may be because the diet of domestic cats usually includes poor-quality meat, as well as other types of food.

The reproductive system is similar to that of many mammals. Like others of the order Carnivora, male cats have permanently descended testicles, and in the penis there is a bone called the baculum. Female cats have up to six pairs of mammary glands. The milk they produce is high in protein, reflecting the high-protein meat diet of adult cats.

11

Spots and stripes

All cats wear beautiful fur coats, and each species displays a unique pattern of spots or stripes, spots and stripes, or no spots or stripes at all.

Fur coats insulate cats from temperature changes, and the longest fur coats, such as those of lynxes and Pallas' cats, are worn by species living in the most extreme environments. But the color and patterning of the coat are designed for camouflage. A cat must conceal itself when stalking prey, and small cats also have to conceal themselves from animals that prey on them. So even if the markings of a cat seem conspicuous to us, they do blend into the cat's natural habitat, making it nearly invisible.

Background color usually matches the colors in the habitat. The pale color of the sand cat, for instance, matches the desert sand. In contrast, spots and stripes tend to break up a cat's outline, making the serval and the wildcat, for instance, less conspicuous in their grassy habitats. The seemingly bold markings of cats

▼ *The claws on this Eurasian lynx's paws are fully protracted, suggesting to us that it is ready to spring into action. Cats' claws are usually kept retracted, protected in a sheath of skin, to keep them sharp.*

▶ *The margay's fur is marked with dark brown or black spots and streaks, so that it disappears from view in the dappled light of rain forests in Central and South America.*

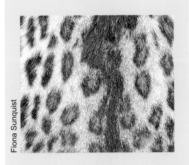

Fiona Sunquist

Did you know?

The fur of the pampas cat of South America can be patterned with gray spots or reddish spots, depending on where it lives. Some pampas cats have been found in forests, but others live in open grasslands.

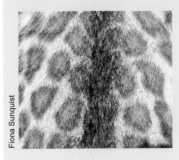

Fiona Sunquist

that live in rain forests, such as the clouded leopard and the ocelot, disappear in the dappled light that filters through the trees.

Some species of cats are wide-ranging and live in lots of different habitats. On them, the coat color and pattern may vary considerably between individuals, depending on their habitat. Pampas cats, for example, can vary in color (see the two photos here), and some individuals have almost no patterning at all. In many species, including the bobcat, margay, ocelot, and serval, a color mutation called melanism produces individual cats that are black all over.

Purposeful paws

All cats have five claws on their forefeet and four on their hindfeet. The first claw on the forefoot, called a dew claw, is very small and does not touch the ground. Most of the time, a cat's claws are retracted into a sheath of skin. This protects them from wear and tear. But when the claws are needed to capture prey or climb a tree, they are protracted by a "jacknife" system of muscles and ligaments in the feet.

Soft pads on the underside of cats' paws give them their legendary quiet movement, which is essential for silently stalking prey. In cats living in very hot climates, such as the desert-living sand cat, the pads are covered with fur to protect them from the ground's heat. Similarly, cats living in very cold climates, such as lynxes, have fur-covered pads to protect them from the cold. The dense fur on the pads also spreads the cat's weight, giving it better footing in desert sand or in snow.

Size and sustenance

People usually split the world's cats into two groups: big and small. But actually cats come in three different sizes: small, medium, and large. Only lions and tigers are truly large. The other "big cats"—cheetahs, pumas, snow leopards, leopards, and jaguars—are medium-sized. And the rest, the cats discussed in this book, are small. As it turns out, a seemingly simple thing like size affects their life in many ways.

▼ *Geoffroy's cat preys on small mammals such as rats, mice, guinea pigs, and agouti. Like most small cats, it takes prey weighing less than 2¼ pounds (1 kilogram).*

Lots of small meals

Cats hunt a wide variety of prey, ranging in size from mouse to buffalo. Small cats, those weighing less than 66 pounds (30 kilograms), eat mainly small rodents (rats, mice, squirrels, etc.), rabbits and hares, and birds. In general, the prey are much smaller than the cats eating them, so small cats must capture several meals each day in order to survive.

In contrast, the medium-sized and large cats prey on bigger animals, such as deer and antelope, and so usually they have to capture a meal only a few times a week. For the large lions and tigers, a steady supply of large prey (usually hoofed mammals) is essential for survival. The medium-sized cats, however, can make it on small prey when larger prey are scarce. Pumas, for instance, prefer deer, and a single kill may last a puma for days or even a couple of weeks. But when deer are scarce, the puma can survive on daily meals of small rodents and birds.

Louise Emmons, an ecologist, has studied the small ocelot and the medium-sized jaguar in a rain forest in Peru. She found that both of these cats hunt a wide assortment of prey, but that the species they hunted were divided according to size: more than 90 percent of the ocelot's prey were small animals weighing less than 2¼ pounds (1 kilogram), while 85 percent of the jaguar's prey were more than 2¼ pounds. Interestingly, South America has only a few big mammals as large as a deer, and no very large ones. This is probably why no large cat lives in South America. A jaguar can survive on a combination of large and fairly small prey, but a lion or tiger cannot.

Up all night

Hunting small prey and needing several meals a day means that small cats are generally more active than big cats. A lion may sleep 17 hours a day after making a large kill, but an ocelot with young may need to hunt for 17 hours a day. Most of the small prey animals are nocturnal, so small cats tend to be active at night. In contrast, about half of the animals that big cats prey on are day-active and half are night-active, and the activity of big cats is timed to match that of their prey.

Small cats compete for small prey with many other predators—such as weasels, hawks, owls, and snakes—and there is always the danger that they themselves will be taken by a predator. Big cats have few competitors and therefore they fear only a very few other species.

Finally, the prey species seem to behave in ways that actually support the needs of their cat predators, although they do not do so willingly! Louise Emmons found that prey species available to ocelots and jaguars were about equally divided in terms of weight, half weighing more than 2¼ pounds (1 kilogram), and half less than 2¼ pounds. She also found that the small rodents and opossums that support ocelots all breed very rapidly. In addition, they breed at an early age, produce several litters of young each year, and the litter size is usually three or more. As a result, there are enough small prey for ocelots to have several meals a day. In contrast, the larger prey all breed rather slowly, with fewer and smaller litters, matching the jaguars' requirements for fewer, but larger meals.

Competition and coexistence

It's easy to see how ocelots and jaguars live in the same areas without conflict: ocelots eat the little things, and jaguars eat the big things. But the ocelot's range also overlaps with that of the margay, the oncilla, and the jaguarundi. How do two or three small cats survive in the same place? How do they all manage to get enough to eat?

▶ *The long-legged serval is a fine hunter. It also digs into the ground to catch prey, and even hooks fish with its paws.*

Sharing

The caracal (right) and the serval are about the same size. They both live in Africa, south of the Sahara desert. But the serval hunts for small rodents (mice and rats) in lush grass along rivers, while the caracal feeds on birds and rodents in more open, drier habitats. In this way, they share the same habitat and avoid competing for the same prey.

They do it by "sharing" the resources of their range in a variety of different ways. The margay, for instance, hunts almost entirely in trees, while the other three hunt mostly on the ground. The largish ocelot probably takes larger prey than the jaguarundi and margay, while the oncilla probably takes the smallest prey. The jaguarundi hunts during the day; the others hunt mostly at night. Jaguarundis also live in more open habitats than the other three species, which always live in densely forested habitats. It seems that two or more species can live together only if they actually somehow live apart. The jaguarundi and the margay, which are similar in size, also differ in coat coloration: jaguarundis are plain, margays are spotted. This also occurs when two species of the same size exist in the same area: the plain Asian golden cat coexists with the spotted fishing cat in Asia; and the plain caracal and the spotted serval coexist in Africa.

Communication among cats

A rub and a scrape, a hiss and a growl—what do they all mean?

The small cats are generally solitary animals. Adults live alone, and usually at some distance from each other. But they still must communicate—with neighbors, with potential mates, and with strangers that trespass on their territories. Females also must communicate with their kittens. Small cats are solitary but not anti-social!

Smelly messages

To communicate at a distance, cats rely on their sense of smell and their ability to produce smelly "messages" in urine, feces, and secretions from glands on various parts of their body. A cat leaves these smelly messages by scent-marking at strategic locations in its territory or home range, where other cats are likely to "read" them.

The scent-marks contain information about the marker's sex and reproductive status. Neighboring cats probably even recognize the individual identity of the scent-marker—one way to tell if a stranger is in the area.

As anyone with a male domestic cat knows, urine-spraying is a common behavior as the cat patrols the boundaries of its home range. Males of most cat species do it. The smell tells other cats, "I'm living here; stay away or risk a fight." Because fights between cats well-armed with sharp teeth and claws are dangerous and potentially fatal, most individuals "respect" the message and stay away.

Another common form of communication is claw-raking, something that a domestic cat may try to do on furniture. When a cat rakes its claws across the bark of a tree it is leaving a

▶ *A serval rakes its claws on the bark of a tree. Claw-raking leaves both a visual sign and an olfactory (smell) message for other servals to let them know that the area is already occupied.*

▼ *Wildcats communicate with each other by smell, sound, and sight. Even solitary cats like these learn to "read" the signs of other animals.*

Angelo Gandolfi

visual signal for other members of its species, as well as an olfactory signal (an odor) from the sweat glands on its paws. Some species scrape or scratch the ground around them after they urinate. These smelly scrapes are also a visual signal of the borders of a cat's home range.

Cats rub various parts of their body against objects in their environment and against other cats. They have glands on their tail, chin, lip, and forehead that leave scent-marks. When cheek-rubbing, cats also leave saliva, another source of olfactory messages. In fact, simply by sniffing a cheek-rubbing, a male domestic cat can tell whether the female who left it is ready to mate or not!

Close encounters

Inevitably, cats do sometimes meet face to face. At close range, their facial expressions, body postures, and vocalizations become important in cat communication. Cats readily display their mood and intentions.

An aggressive cat, for instance, threatens another cat by turning its erect ears so that the back of the ears face the other animal. At the same time the aggressor stands with its back parallel to the ground as its tail thrashes from side to side. Sometimes a low growl can be heard.

A submissive cat is equally easy to spot. It flattens its ears to the side, its pupils become dilated, and it crouches down, slinks away, or even rolls over on its back. Hissing is the usual sound made by this cat.

Encounters between cats aren't always hostile. For example, when a male and a female, who is ready to mate, come together, mutual neck-rubbing shows their friendly intentions. And, of course, the familiar "meow" and purr are anything but hostile. Soft meows are heard in interactions between a mother and her kittens. And louder meows are used by adults to attract mates. Purring is also most common between mothers and kittens and is a sign of contentment.

A rub and a scrape, a hiss and a growl—in the language of cats their meanings are clear, at least to other cats.

To bury or not to bury

People offer their house cat a litter box so that the cat can bury its feces. Many species of small cats in the wild also bury their feces, but big cats do not. Feces contains scent information for other cats in the area, and burying it may prevent a cat's message from reaching the nose of another—for instance, a big cat that might prey on a small one. Among domestic cats that have been abandoned and are now feral (wild), dominant cats do not bury their feces, but low-ranking cats do. And the lynx will bury its feces within its territory but leave it uncovered along the borders.

▶ *A hostile cat. At close range, cats display their emotions through the position of their ears, the dilation or contraction of the pupils of their eyes, and the baring of their sharp teeth.*

The hunters

Cats are sometimes described as "perfect killing machines," but they are not born with the skills they will need to hunt and kill their prey. Cats must learn to hunt and to kill, and it takes a long time for them to get the hang of it.

Learning to hunt

The learning process begins long before kittens are weaned, with a simple lesson from their mother. She kills a prey animal and takes it back to the den so that the kittens can watch her eat it. Then, when the kittens are a little older and ready for solid foods, she leaves dead prey for the kittens to eat. Next, she begins to bring live prey to her young so they can try to kill it themselves. She helps by re-capturing prey that escape the kittens' clumsy attacks. This gives them practice in the hardest part of hunting: making the killing bite.

Throughout this period, kittens are also getting essential practice through their lively play. They vigorously chase, stalk, and pounce on each other, taking turns in the roles of hunter and hunted. Kittens also play with their mother and with anything else that strikes their fancy. They stalk and pounce on swaying blades of grass or a rustling leaf, rehearsing the skills they will need to survive on their own.

At about three months of age (in most small cats), kittens begin to follow their mother on hunting trips. On these trips, they gradually improve and refine their skills.

The learning process is fairly slow. Even when young cats finally leave their mothers, usually at about one year of age, they have yet to become "perfect killing machines." For a young cat, the next few months may be the hardest of its life as it struggles on its own to find enough prey to survive.

▲ *The fishing cat lives near water and uses its paws to scoop out fish.*
▼ *The jungle cat lives in Europe, Africa, and Asia, and hunts rodents and other small animals.*

▲ *This ocelot's crouching posture and fixed, staring eyes reveal that it is stalking prey.*

▼ *The Eurasian lynx is a solitary hunter. It's main diet is rabbit and hare, but it also hunts many other small animals.*

How cats hunt

All cats, large and small, use similar techniques to capture prey. The hunt begins when the cat spots a potential creature of prey—a mouse or an unwary bird. Most cats hunt by sight, but a few species, such as the serval, also use hearing to detect prey. With the prey in its sights, the cat then begins its slow and cautious stalk. Using all available cover—a patch of tall grass, a pile of rocks, or even the shadows of thick bushes—the cat moves closer and closer toward its goal. Its posture is unmistakable: ears flattened, eyes unblinking, body crouched low, and every muscle tense, ready to freeze if there is any sign of wariness in the prey.

Then, when it has narrowed the distance to the unsuspecting prey, the cat bursts into a speeding rush to reach it, pounces, and grabs the prey with its front paws. Finally, with the prey in its grasp, the cat delivers the killing bite, usually to the neck, where the cat's powerful canine teeth break the victim's neck or pierce its skull. To kill larger prey, cats such as clouded leopards may forego the neck bite, instead clamping their jaws across the prey's throat to suffocate it. Small cats also sometimes repeatedly bite and shake their prey until it dies.

Of course, there are variations to this typical hunting sequence. The fishing cat may wait watchfully on a riverbank and snag fish with its claws. A caracal sometimes leaps into the air to pluck birds in flight. Most small cats can snag prey as it emerges from an underground burrow. The serval even uses its front feet to deliver a blow to the prey that will stun or kill it.

This brings us to the three basic hunting styles of cats. Cats may adopt a mobile hunting strategy, moving slowly throughout their home range, actively searching for a potential meal. When the cat finds it, the "stalk, pounce, and kill" sequence is set in motion. Cats may also employ an ambush strategy—they simply wait patiently for prey to emerge from a burrow or otherwise cross their path, and then grab it. Finally, cats may simply stumble onto something to eat in the course of their travels—and catch it any way they can.

All cats seem to use a combination of these hunting styles, but some, like the serval, are noted for being ambush predators. The serval uses a unique "dig and wait" technique to catch African mole-rats, which live in long, underground tunnels. After finding a tunnel, the serval digs a hole into it, then sits and waits, with one paw raised. Mole-rats always rush to repair any breach in their tunnels, and the serval is ready for them. At the first sign of a mole-rat, the serval hooks the animal with one paw, flings it away, then pounces before it knows what hit it. Like the fishing cat, a serval can also hook fish out of water.

Ocelots combine mobile hunting and ambush hunting. When using the ambush strategy, an ocelot moves to one spot and sits and waits for as long as an hour or more. Then it quickly goes to another site and waits again. When moving between ambush sites, the ocelot's behavior is quite different from its behavior during mobile hunting: It travels two or three times faster. When it is mobile hunting it moves slowly, constantly watching and listening for prey.

Eurasian lynxes

The word *lynx* comes from the Greek word meaning "to see." Lynxes hunt by sight and are reported to be able to see a mouse at 250 feet (75 meters), a hare at 1000 feet (300 meters), and a roe deer at 1600 feet (500 meters). But the lynx itself is seldom seen.

Across Europe and Asia

The secretive Eurasian lynx haunts the forests of Europe, from Scandinavia to the Mediterranean, and across Russia and other countries of the former Soviet Union, as far as Mongolia and Manchuria in northern Asia. It also lives in Turkey, Iraq, and Iran. Its preferred habitat is forest with plenty of dense cover, but across the vast Asian continent the lynx can also live in rocky areas, open forests, and even in scrub.

The Eurasian lynx is among the largest of the small cats, with a powerful body set on long, sturdy legs. Some individuals weigh as much as 84 pounds (38 kilograms) although the average weight is about half this amount: 44 pounds (20 kilograms) for males, and 37 pounds (17 kilograms) for females.

The lone hunter

Rabbits and hares form a large part of the diet of the Eurasian lynx. But lynxes are capable of taking far bigger prey when it is available. In some parts of Europe and Asia, lynxes take considerable numbers of roe deer, and there are reports of lynxes hunting animals as large as yaks in Tibet. If necessary, they will prey on small creatures such as mice, marmots, and game birds. And, unfortunately, lynxes are not opposed to a meal of sheep or goat, which inevitably puts them into conflict with farmers.

Each adult lives alone on a home range (a territory) that varies in size from 11 to 300 square kilometers (4 to 115 square miles). The size depends on the abundance of prey; when prey animals are scarce, lynxes have to search over larger areas to find enough to eat.

A male's home range will generally overlap the area occupied by at least one female. Male and female come together briefly to mate in the early spring, and the female gives birth to one to five kittens about ten weeks later. The kittens are weaned at about five months of age but stay with their mother until the next mating season. This timing is probably critical to the survival of the young lynx, because prey animals are usually less abundant in winter and are harder to capture in the deep snow. The young lynx does not have to truly fend for itself until spring, when more prey are available and it is easier for an inexperienced hunter to kill.

Predators and hunters

Aside from people, wolves are the Eurasian lynx's only predators. Competing for similar prey, lynxes and wolves are "natural enemies," and wolves seem to win. When we read historical reports we learn that when wolf populations increased, lynxes rapidly declined or even disappeared from an area.

For centuries, people hunted down Eurasian lynxes, especially in densely populated parts of Europe. People considered them vermin—vicious predators that raided stockyards and reduced the number of game animals such as roe deer, which people prized as food. Lynxes suffered from being hunted for their fur and also when the forests were chopped down. By the beginning of this century they had been drastically reduced or eliminated throughout Europe.

In this century, however, people's attitudes have changed. The number of lynxes is increasing and they are re-colonizing their former haunts. Programs to reintroduce lynxes into various parts of their range are also under way.

▼ *A Eurasian lynx in a Swiss cornfield. Reintroducing cats to the wild will always be controversial because few remaining natural habitats are very far from some sort of human settlement. A deep-seated fear of cats killing livestock—or attacking people—is hard to overcome, especially because cats do sometimes take farm animals and attack people.*

Urs Breitenmoser

▲ *By the beginning of this century the lynx was extinct in Switzerland. It was reintroduced in 1976, and its numbers are now growing.*

▶ *The Eurasian lynx's paws are large and, in winter, so thickly furred that they serve as snow shoes, making it easy for the lynx to travel over crusty snow. This is when lynxes find it easiest to prey on deer, whose hooves break through the snow, hampering their movement and their ability to escape a stalking cat.*

The last lynx in Switzerland was killed in 1872, 1894, or 1902, depending on who is judging the reliability of the records. Whatever the date, lynxes had become extinct in Switzerland, as they had through much of western Europe. But between 1971 and 1976, 20 lynxes from Czechoslovakia were released into Switzerland, and since then the lynx population has grown to about 100 animals. They occupy about 4000 square miles (10,000 square kilometers) in the Alps and 2000 square miles (5000 square kilometers) in the Jura Mountains.

A success story

This female lynx (pictured with her cubs) was part of the Swiss reintroduction program. Where European lynxes are protected they survive and reproduce as long as suitable habitat and prey animals are available.

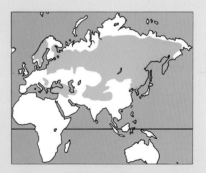

The reintroduction of lynxes was controversial—farmers worried about the cats killing sheep, and hunters worried about them taking too many roe deer and chamois—but their fears turned out to be unjustified. At first the released lynxes hunted over very small areas and killed many roe deer and chamois, which were easy to catch because they were unused to predators. But as the prey became more wary, the lynxes were forced to greatly expand their home ranges to hunt successfully. As a result, in Switzerland there is no more than one lynx, on average, per 40 square miles (1 per 100 square kilometers). At this density, the local people are more tolerant of the lynxes taking a few sheep and deer.

21

A question of relationships

Spanish lynx and caracal: How are they related? Scientists are still working it out. The Spanish lynx lives in a tiny area of Portugal and Spain while the caracal has a wider habitat.

Spanish lynx

Some scientists believe that the Spanish lynx is merely a subspecies of the Eurasian lynx. Others argue that it is different enough to be called a separate species. So far, there's no conclusive evidence to end the debate, but in this book we treat the Spanish lynx as a species with its own scientific name, *Lynx pardinus*.

In many features it does differ from the Eurasian lynx. First, it is much smaller. Males weigh about 28 pounds (13 kilograms), and females are slightly smaller. The Spanish lynx's coat is more heavily spotted, and the spots are darker than those of the Eurasian lynx. But both species have similar long legs, short tails, and tufted ears. Their social, reproductive, and hunting behavior is also nearly identical.

In danger of extinction

The Spanish lynx is one of Europe's most endangered mammals. Once found throughout Spain and Portugal, it now survives only in remote mountain regions and among the sand dunes and scrub in southern Spain. Like Eurasian lynxes, the Spanish lynx has declined because of overhunting and loss of habitat.

The Spanish lynx specializes in eating rabbits. In fact, scientists found the remains of rabbits in nearly 90 percent of the scats (dried feces) they examined. In contrast, ducks and other birds, the second most common food items, were found in only about 20 percent of the scats. But we know that the Spanish lynxes also eat a variety of other mammals, from small mice and rats to red deer, fallow deer, and wild boar. Like other lynxes, the Spanish lynx takes whatever is abundant and easily caught.

▲ The Spanish lynx inhabits open forests, thickets, and sand dunes and scrub. It is endangered, and it survives only in areas remote from human activity.

◄ The word caracal *is from a Turkish word meaning "black-ear." The caracal's plain reddish coat is marked only by white fur on the chin, throat, and belly, and by black-backed ears and ear tufts. Because they don't have spots, caracals are seldom hunted for their fur.*

Caracal

No one argues about whether or not the caracal is a species—but whether it is truly a member of the lynx group or just happens to look like a lynx is an open question. At present, its scientfic name is *Lynx caracal*.

Like lynxes, the caracal is a robust, medium-sized cat, weighing up to 33 pounds (15 kilograms), with a short tail and tufted ears. Unlike the true lynxes, the caracal has short fur, which is unspotted, and it does not possess a facial ruff.

Caracals live in dry habitats throughout Africa south of the Sahara desert, in parts of the Middle East, and across Central Asia as far as Pakistan and northern India. They hunt mostly at night, and what they hunt for depends on where they live.

In Central Asia, a study of caracals showed that about half of their diet was hares, supplemented by sand rats, jerboas, and ground squirrels. In South Africa, however, the caracal's favorite foods are the rock hyrax (a small mammal) and the mountain reedbuck (a medium-sized antelope). The remains of these two animals were found in 73 percent of caracal scats. Bits of rabbits and hares were found in only 10 percent of the scats. In other places where caracals live, their diet is likely to be quite different.

Caracals seem to be typical solitary cats, with the only social groups being mothers and their young. Little is known, however, about the details of their behavior and reproduction.

Cat among the pigeons

Caracals are easily tamed, and people used to train them for hunting birds and hares. In India, caracals were put into an arena with a flock of pigeons, and men took bets on how many pigeons the cats could bring down before the birds flew off. This is where the expression "to put a cat among the pigeons" comes from.

◀ *The Spanish lynx has a beautifully patterned coat. It is now endangered, and lives only in southwestern Spain and in Portugal.*

North American lynxes

A fluctuating population

Ernest Thompson Seton, a naturalist who wrote many stories about wild animals, was observing the essential relationship between the North American lynx and snowshoe hares. The lynx eats other things, of course—from mice and squirrels to grouse, and even deer and caribou fawns—but snowshoe hares are its main prey.

In fact, the numbers of lynxes and hares in Canada seem to follow a ten-year cycle, with lynx numbers shadowing those of hares. Every ten years or so, populations of showshoe hares drop suddenly, for unknown reasons, perhaps related to changes in their food supply. Lynxes have to search over larger areas to find enough to eat. Lynx females have difficulty feeding themselves, so they cannot raise as many young, or they fail to reproduce at all. Many lynxes starve. Soon after snowshoe hare numbers drop, so do lynx numbers.

Gradually, however, snowshoe hare populations begin to recover, and then the lynx

▼ *The North American lynx specializes in hunting snowshoe hares. The lynx's very broad, snowshoelike paws make it as swift in the snow as the hare, but even so, for every five hares a lynx chases, four will manage to escape.*

population increases. When the hare population reaches its peak, lynxes reproduce more successfully and become abundant. Then, once again, the hare population crashes, and the cycle begins anew.

Smaller than its cousins

Excluding its short tail, the North American lynx is 32 to 39 inches (80 to 100 centimeters) long. With an average weight of 18 to 22 pounds (8 to 10 kilograms), the North American lynx is smaller than the Eurasian lynx, but otherwise very similar in appearance and behavior. Some scientists even believe that the North American lynx belongs to the same species as the Eurasian lynx (along with the Spanish lynx), and that differences between them have developed simply as a result of the different habitats they live in. Other scientists believe that the differences are now so great that it is a separate species, which they call *Lynx canadensis* (as we do in this book). Although

lynxes are among the best-studied of all the small cats, much remains to be learned about them to resolve this debate.

Distribution

Today, the North American lynx is distributed throughout the forests of Canada and Alaska, and in a few mountainous areas in the north of the United States. During the first half of this century lynxes were eliminated in most of the northern parts of the United States where they had previously lived, and their numbers in southern Canada were greatly reduced. This happened for two reasons: trapping (for their fur) killed too many of them, and their wilderness areas were taken over by human settlers.

More recently, however, lynx numbers have increased and now seem stable. Trapping is carefully regulated, and at present the North American lynx is not considered threatened or endangered.

Bobcats

Bobcats have a reputation for being adaptable. They feed on quite a wide variety of prey, and they live in many types of habitats. But can they avoid the people who want to kill them for their fur?

◀ *About twice the size of a domestic cat, the male bobcat weighs 22 pounds (10 kilograms) and females 15 pounds (7 kilograms) on average. They are the smallest of all the lynx species—and the most adaptable in both their habitat and their diet.*

Home, home on the range

The bobcat is the most adaptable species of lynx. It has a wide distribution in North America, ranging from coast to coast and from northern Mexico to the border between the United States and Canada. It is at home in a variety of habitats from the coastal marshes of Georgia and the deserts of Arizona to the woods of Maine and the mountains of Montana. Bobcats do not survive, however, in areas of intensive farming in the Midwest, and the spreading suburbs are driving them out of other areas.

Wherever they live, bobcats generally live alone. Males and females meet briefly, once a year between December and April, for mating. Then they go their separate ways. Nine or ten weeks later, kittens are born in a cave, under a rock ledge, or in a brush pile where the female has fashioned a nest. As many as six kittens, but usually no more than two to four, make up a litter. Born blind and helpless, the kittens open their eyes after nine or ten days and they mature quickly.

Kittens start to eat meat in their second month and are weaned from milk after three or four months. But they stay with their mother, learning about their environment and practicing their hunting

skills, until their mother breeds again the next spring. Then they must find a home of their own.

Young males usually travel far and wide to find an unoccupied home range—one where no other male bobcat is already living. Females often settle near their mother, or take part of her home range. These exclusive home ranges vary in size from about half a square mile (1 square kilometer) to 16 square miles (42 square kilometers). Adult males have a larger home range than females do, and it usually overlaps the ranges of two or more females. Except for mating, however, male and female bobcats avoid one another by not using the same parts of the range at the same time.

How do they do this? Probably by making scent-marks. As a bobcat moves along a trail in its home range, it stops and sprays smelly urine on trees and other vegetation. In one study, scientists discovered that bobcats sprayed as often as seven times for each kilometer they walked. Bobcats also deposit their feces in one site or a few sites, creating smelly latrines. The smell of a bobcat's fresh urine or feces is like a stop sign to other bobcats. It tells them that a bobcat is already using the area

▶ *A bobcat rests in a bird's nest. Bobcats spend most of their time on the ground, but they sometimes climb trees to escape their predators.*

Marty Cordano/DRK Photo

and, unless they want a fight, they should back off.

These smells also contain messages about a bobcat's sex, reproductive condition, and even individual identity. Without ever meeting face to face, bobcats know their neighbors, and a male can tell when a female is ready to mate. Despite their solitary nature, bobcats (and most other cats as well) have a rich social life—but only at a distance, communicating with others in the language of odors.

▼ *The bobcat gets its name from its short tail, which is only about 6 inches (15 centimeters) long. Some people also called it the bay lynx.*

A fleeting glimpse

"It was actually just a blur shooting across the path in front of me, but I knew instantly that I had finally seen my first wild bobcat. Or had I really seen anything? The mind does play tricks. However, apparitions don't leave tracks, and the spoor [tracks] confirmed my sighting. During the next six years of research on this species, I was privileged to observe many bobcats, but what I still remember most is that first meeting."

Bobcat expert S. Douglas Miller's first encounter with North America's most abundant wild cat is typical. Few people ever catch more than a fleeting glimpse of this secretive cat, with its short "bobtail," ruffed face, and spotted coat. Undoubtedly, it avoids people, who are its main predators.

Bobcats as hunters

It is dawn, and a hungry bobcat has sighted a cottontail rabbit foraging in the snow. Slowly, slowly, it begins to stalk a meal. Concealing itself behind rocks or in the shadow of a tree, the bobcat tries to get close enough to strike. When it is about 33 feet (10 meters) away from the still-unsuspecting rabbit, the bobcat takes off. With a bounding rush, it covers the remaining distance and pounces at its prey. But the rabbit gets away. The bobcat must hunt again.

Most attempts, about five out of six, are unsuccessful. Not having great speed, the bobcat will rarely pursue a rabbit—or any other prey animal—if it escapes the bobcat's first pounce. Instead, the cat will look for another chance to capture a meal.

Bobcats choose from a large menu of prey—during the period of a year, a bobcat may eat 45 different items—but they specialize in capturing rabbits and hares. Thirteen different species of rabbits and hares live in various parts of the bobcat's North American home, and these are the staples of the bobcat's diet. On average, one medium-sized rabbit a day is what a bobcat needs to survive.

Bobcats can't always manage to get a bunny a day, however, so they also take large numbers of mice, rats, and squirrels, and aren't above making a meal of a bird, a fish, or a large insect. Yet, bobcats also take large animals, such as deer, when they can. They are most likely to capture them during the late winter and spring. In winter, the deer are stressed and their movements are hampered by deep snow, making it easier for the bobcat to capture them. In spring, newborn deer are fairly easy prey.

When dealing with small and medium-sized prey, a bobcat pounces, grabs the animal with its front paws, and delivers a killing bite to the back of its neck. Deer pose a different challenge: an adult deer may be seven or eight times heavier than the bobcat. Bobcats are most successful when deer are bedded down. Pouncing on the deer, the bobcat bites through its throat and windpipe. It then holds onto the deer's throat with its teeth until the animal suffocates.

Predators of bobcats

The bobcat does have enemies. Pumas, wolves, and dogs will kill adult bobcats; and bobcat kittens may fall victim to eagles and other large birds of prey. But the bobcat's greatest predators are people. In many parts of the United States, bounties were offered for dead bobcats because they occasionally preyed on domestic chickens and livestock. And since the mid-1970s—when trade in the fur of tigers and the spotted big cats was curtailed—harvesting bobcats for their fur has been a growth industry; between 60 000 and 80 000 bobcats per year have been slaughtered to make fur coats.

Right now, bobcats seem to be holding their own, despite being "harvested" for their fur, and despite the depletion of their wilderness habitats during the past 200 years. How long they can withstand these pressures remains to be seen.

Len-Lee-Rue/Image Bank

▲ *The bobcat is about twice as big as a domestic cat. It lives in an area stretching from southern Canada to Mexico.*

▶ *A bobcat dashes up to catch a muskrat, which has left the safety of its watery home. Bobcats prefer rabbits and hares, but any small mammal will do in a pinch.*

◀ *Using its paws, the bobcat flips the muskrat over so that it cannot escape. Only one in six attempts to catch prey is successful—usually prey manage to escape the bobcat's first pounce, and bobcats rarely try to chase down an escapee.*

Bobcats and rabbits

Rabbits breed like, well, rabbits. In regular cycles, rabbit populations grow very large, very quickly, then crash dramatically, for unknown reasons. Bobcat populations follow these cycles. When rabbit numbers crash, bobcat mothers may abandon their kittens, and young females may postpone breeding. Sometimes, bobcats may change from their solitary lifestyle and gather together in small groups in the areas where there is an abundance of rabbits.

▲ *The bobcat holds the muskrat in its paws and prepares to deliver a killing bite to the back of its neck. Sharp, canine teeth pierce through the muskrat's neck vertebrae.*

Servals

The serval is a tall, long-legged cat, described as the cat world's version of a giraffe. While most cats move their compact bodies in a low crouched posture, the serval stalks as if on stilts through the grass and seems to be stretched as tall as possible.

▼ *The long-legged serval specializes in catching rats.*

Walking tall

The serval has a very long neck reaching to a slim face topped by large ears. It also has the longest legs of any member of the cat family, and like giraffes, its front legs are far longer than its hind legs.

Weighing between 18 and 40 pounds (about 8 to 18 kilograms), a serval may stand up to 24 inches (60 centimeters) at the shoulder. In comparison, an ocelot of similar weight would be 16 inches (about 40 centimeters) at the shoulder. The serval's unusual body plan reflects its unusual hunting style, which is adapted to hunting mole-rats and other rodents by sound in the grassland. For more on this topic, see pages 18–19.

At home in Africa

Servals live in grasslands and open woodlands in Africa, south of the Sahara desert, but always in areas with plenty of water. In the past, servals also lived in the Atlas Mountains region of northern Africa, but no one has seen them there for more than 20 years.

Elsewhere in Africa, people sometimes hunt servals for their spotted fur but the hunting pressure has never been intense. Servals also get shot occasionally for preying on domestic chickens. But they seem to be able to survive living quite close to people in rural areas. In fact, they may thrive on the increased number of rats and mice that come with the creation of farms. Today, servals are one of the few cat species not in serious danger of extinction.

A solitary life after 12 months

Like most cats, servals are solitary hunters. Females that were studied in Kenya lived on home ranges at least 3 1/2 square miles (9 square kilometers) in size, while the males had larger home ranges that overlapped the ranges of two or more females. Each serval scent-marks its range to avoid living and hunting in the same areas at the same time. The scent-marks of females probably also tell males when they are ready to mate.

▶ *Ears pricked, a serval listens for approaching prey.*

Servals are very good hunters, maybe the best in the cat world. While some cats are successful in just one of every five or ten attempts to kill prey, servals make a kill in about half of all tries. Servals may therefore be a great help to their human neighbors by killing many rat and mice pests. If people can learn to live with servals in their midst—and balance the loss of a few chickens with the serval's positive contribution to rodent pest control—this unusual "giraffe cat" will survive.

▼ *A serval bares its sharp teeth.*

A. Bannister/NHPA

Here are two mysterious beauties of Southeast Asia. One is the size of a small leopard; the other is the size of a domestic cat.

The clouded leopard

The clouded leopard is known to scientists as *Neofelis nebulosa*, "the new cat with cloudy fur." Its beautiful coat pattern—with large, dark, cloudlike markings that turn into spots on its head, legs, and belly—is just one of this mysterious cat's amazing features. About the size of a small leopard, the clouded leopard weighs up to 48 pounds (22 kilograms) and measures about 6½ feet (2 meters)—but almost half of this is an extraordinarily long tail! For its size, it has larger canine teeth than any other species of cat in the world. Short, powerful legs give it an unusual slouching gait.

Clouded leopards live in forests in Asia, and because they are rarely seen, people once believed that they lived and hunted only in trees. In fact, Malayans call them *rimau dahan*, meaning "tree tiger." Clouded leopards frequently rest in trees and are good climbers, well-adapted for hunting in trees. But they may also hunt on the ground.

Clouded leopards are found in Nepal and northeast India, across southern Asia to the south of China and Taiwan, and southwards to Malaysia, and the islands of Sumatra and Borneo. In Borneo, where they are the largest predator, clouded leopards feed on large prey such as pigs and deer—animals they must hunt on the ground. But in many other places, these prey are taken by tigers and leopards, so the clouded leopard feeds on tree-living monkeys and birds. Spending more time in the trees may also offer the clouded leopard some protection from the larger predators.

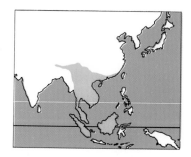

▼ *The clouded leopard uses its long, bushy tail to help it balance when climbing trees or walking along limbs.*

Varin/Visage/AUSCAPE

Information from zoo animals

Nothing is known about the clouded leopard's social system or behavior in the wild, but it probably has a solitary life except when breeding. In zoos, however, males often kill a female when, in her reproductive cycle, she is ready to mate. Pairing has more chance of success if a male and female are introduced when they are less than six months old.

The two animals then form a strong pair bond and stay together for life. Whether this unusual cat also has an unusual social life in the wild remains to be seen.

The marbled cat

The marbled cat is similar to the clouded leopard, and even less is known about it. It is about the size of a domestic cat, weighing from 4½ to 11 pounds (2 to 5 kilograms), but its

▶ *The thick soft fur of the marbled cat varies in color from brownish gray to yellow and reddish brown and is marked with large blotches, spots, and stripes.*

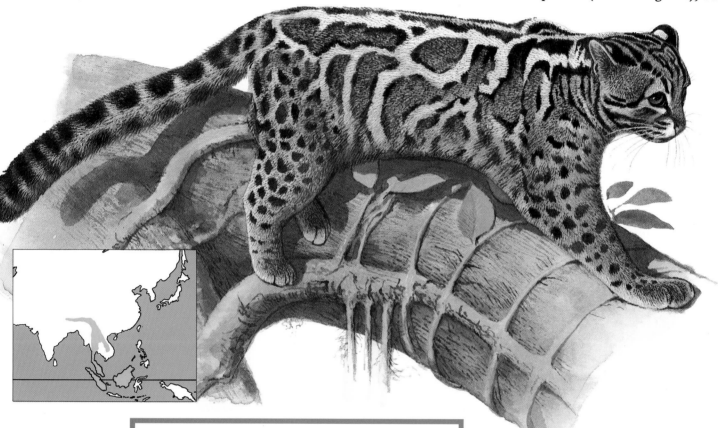

Studying the marbled cat

Rare in the wild, marbled cats are also rare in zoos. Perhaps only a half-dozen of these cats are in zoo collections worldwide. By studying these animals, and recording their habits in captivity, scientists can learn much about the way these animals behave in the wild.

Rod Williams/Bruce Coleman Ltd.

thick fur and long tail make it look larger. The marbled cat's tail is one of the longest, for its body size, of any cat.

Marbled cats live in forests in Asia, from Nepal through southeastern Asia to Borneo and Sumatra. They hunt in trees for birds, but also eat squirrels, rats, and frogs. It is interesting that, like clouded leopards, marbled cats in Borneo may spend more time on the ground than marbled cats do in other parts of their range. Marbled cats are probably solitary and nocturnal.

Endangered species

The clouded leopard and the marbled cat, despite their small size, are fairly closely related to the big *Panthera* cats such as the tiger and the leopard. Some scientists believe that the marbled cat's form may resemble the forest-dwelling ancestors of big cats, which lived 10 million years ago.

Always rare, clouded leopards and marbled cats are now endangered. They are suffering primarily from the loss of their tropical forest habitat, which is being cleared for farms. Clouded leopards are thought to be extinct on the island of Taiwan.

The extraordinary fishing cat

This unusual cat from Asia is a good swimmer and enjoys a fish for dinner.

At home in the water

The large and robust fishing cat lives in tropical Asia, including southwest India, Sri Lanka, the southern Himalayas, Bangladesh, Burma, Vietnam, southern China, Java, Sumatra, and Thailand. But within this broad range, it is found only in wetland habitats. It chooses areas with thick cover near water—in marshes, mangrove forests, and vegetated strips along rivers and streams.

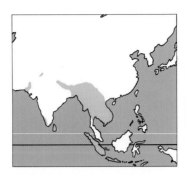

▲ *From a log jutting out over the water, the fishing cat watches, alert and ready to pounce.*

▲ *The fishing cat seizes its prey with its paws.*

Why only wetlands? Because this extraordinary cat actually fishes! Fish and other water-living creatures such as snakes and snails are a major part of the fishing cat's diet. Some people have reported seeing a fishing cat make a deep dive to catch prey. More often, the cat crouches at the water's edge on a rock or sandbank, waits for a fish or some other animal, then grabs it with its paws. It can also scoop prey out of the water with a front paw or catch the prey in its mouth. It hunts small mammals and birds as well, if they are near water.

Unfortunately, little else is known about this remarkable cat in the wild. There are probably about 30 individuals in zoos; and from them we know that, after a successful mating between a male and female, the female is pregnant for three months, then gives birth to two or three kittens. The mother nurses her young until they are about six months old. By about $8\frac{1}{2}$ months of age they reach the size of adults, which is $25\frac{1}{2}$ to $33\frac{1}{2}$ inches (65 to 85 centimeters) head and body length. Fishing cats probably live alone in the wild, but in zoos these cats are remarkably tolerant of others. Several adult fishing cats will live peacefully in the same exhibit.

▲ *The fishing cat clamps the fish (now dead) in its jaws ready to eat.*

A cat that likes water

Some cats hate water. But not the fishing cat! It is a strong swimmer, and its front paws are partly webbed. It has shorter legs than most cats, and is thicker and less elegant than many other species. The fishing cat's body is well adapted to its way of life. It is a good swimmer and a good hunter. It catches prey both on land and in the water—which certainly increases its chances of finding a good meal.

Two golden cats and a leopard cat

When you read the names of these three cats you may think their colors (and patterns) are predictable. In fact, they have coats of many colors.

Close relatives, far apart

The African golden cat is a creature of the high rain forest and moist woodland of West and Central Africa. Surprisingly, its closest relatives live some 4300 miles (7000 kilometers) away. The Asian golden cat inhabits tropical rain forests and deciduous forests in Southeast Asia, from Nepal to China, and southwards through Burma, Thailand, Malaysia, and Sumatra. Some scientists think that a long time ago a belt of moist forest existed from Africa to tropical Asia, and golden cats lived throughout it. But later, when the climate became drier in the middle parts of this huge area, the golden cats were separated geographically by vast deserts and evolved into two species.

Despite their names, the African golden cat and the Asian golden cat have variable coat colorings and markings. In fact, the African golden cat has one of the most variable coat

◀ *People in Liberia call the African golden cat "the leopard's little brother."*

▼ *The leopard cat is about the same size as a large domestic cat. It is common through much of Asia.*

Jean-Paul Ferrero/AUSCAPE

36

Fire tiger

In Thailand, the word for the Asian golden cat means "fire tiger." Some Thai people believe that burning the fur of a golden cat will scare away a nearby tiger. The Karen people of Thailand believe that carrying a single hair of the golden cat will keep tigers away. Other villagers cook the golden cat, fur and all; eating this is supposed to keep all wild animals from attacking.

► *The Asian golden cat is also known as Temminck's cat. It was named in 1828 after C. J. Temminck, a Dutch naturalist who in 1827 first scientifically described and named the African golden cat.*

▼ *The Chinese name for the leopard cat is the "money cat" because its many spots remind people of Chinese coins. All leopard cats are spotted, but spot patterns are variable. Background coloration also varies greatly, from pale yellow, to gray, and rich red.*

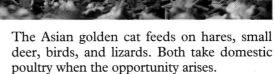

The Asian golden cat feeds on hares, small deer, birds, and lizards. Both take domestic poultry when the opportunity arises.

Female golden cats give birth to one or two young at a time, but little more is known about their breeding or social behavior. They are probably solitary in the wild.

A tolerant cat

The adaptable leopard cat is one of Asia's most common and widespread cats. It lives in Pakistan, India, the southern Himalayas, Bangladesh, Burma, Thailand, Vietnam, Malaysia, Indonesia, and parts of China. Leopard cats are at home in many types of habitat, from tropical rain forests to cool pine forests and even semi-desert. People do not seem to bother them much, and they are often found near villages in agricultural areas. As a result, the leopard cat is among the few cats species not considered to be endangered.

This small cat, weighing from $6\frac{1}{2}$ to $15\frac{1}{2}$ pounds (3 to 7 kilograms), hunts on the ground and in trees, usually at night. It seems to be a good swimmer and may sometimes be found in caves. These versatile abilities allow it to have a diverse diet of hares, rodents (rats, mice, etc.), reptiles (lizards, snakes), birds, fish, and cave-living bats. It probably lives a solitary life, except when mating.

The female leopard cat gives birth to two or three young, in a hollow tree, small cave, or the shelter of a fallen tree trunk. The young reach maturity at about 18 months of age. Although leopard cats are very common in Asia, scientists still have much to learn.

colorings of any cat species. All-black golden cats of both species are also sometimes seen.

At between 26 and 33 pounds (12 to 15 kilograms), the Asian golden cat is larger than its African cousin, which varies in weight from 11 to 26 pounds (5 to 12 kilograms). Both species are thought to hunt mainly on the ground at dawn and dusk and during the night. The African golden cat eats rats, mice, hyraxes, monkeys, and duikers (small antelopes), and probably birds.

Ocelots

This beautiful spotted cat lives in forested habitats along with five of its "cousins": jaguars, pumas, margays, oncillas, and jaguarundis. The ocelot is the third largest cat among the forest-dwellers.

Central and South America

The northernmost part of the ocelot's range is Texas, near the Mexican border. Populations are scattered through Mexico and Central America, to as far south as Argentina in South America. With its dappled coat blending into the background, the ocelot lives by hunting small animals in the forest and woodland and other places with lots of bushes. It relies on dense cover to hide its approach to prey, and the dense cover may also shelter the ocelot from its predators, which may include jaguars and pumas as well as people.

There are other cats around, too. In fact, the ocelot is the third largest cat after the jaguar and the puma. Male ocelots weigh between 20 and 28 pounds (9 to 13 kilograms) and measure 33 to 39 inches (85 to 100 centimeters) head-body length; the females are slightly smaller. What's surprising, given their size, is that most of their prey weigh less than 2¼ pounds (1 kilogram), although they do sometimes

▼ *An aggressive face for the photographer. Ocelots may be threatened by crab-eating foxes and other predators, but their greatest enemies are probably people who hunt them with dogs.*

Jany Sauvanet/NHPA

Roguenant/Jacana

▲ *The usual litter size for ocelots is just one kitten. A mother stays near her kitten in the den for a few days after its birth, leaving only to drink and hunt nearby.*

Did you know?

Until trade was banned, ocelot skins formed a large part of the fur trade in the 1960s. In 1970, 140,000 ocelot skins were legally imported into the United States alone. Some illegal trade in ocelot skins continues, but is greatly reduced, partly because ocelots are becoming rarer and harder to find.

Ron Austing

take slightly larger prey. The ocelot's favorite prey seems to be rodents such as rats, mice, and agouti, but their diet also includes birds, fish, snakes, lizards, and land crabs.

The ocelot hunts on the ground, even though it may spend some time resting in a tree during the day. It usually hunts at night, but hunting may continue into the daylight hours, especially if it is cloudy or rainy. A female ocelot with young also has to extend her hunting hours to find enough food to support herself and her growing kittens. Scientists tracked one female ocelot in Peru who was hunting 17 hours a day when her kittens were about a month old—and the kittens still died, probably of starvation. Even without young to feed, female ocelots may need to hunt for up to 12 hours a day to survive on their rodent prey.

One kitten

The difficulty of finding food may explain why ocelots usually give birth to just one kitten at a time. Young ocelots also mature more slowly than many other small cats. A kitten depends on its mother for five or six months and does not leave its mother's home range until it is about two years old.

The social life of ocelots is typical of solitary cats. The female lives alone, except when she has a kitten, on a home range that varies in size from about 1 to 4 square miles (2 to 10 square kilometers). The home ranges of neighboring females do not overlap. The male's home range is about 2 to 7 square miles (5 to 18 square kilometers) and overlaps the ranges of one or more females. Males and females hunt alone but know their neighbors by sight and smell. And in some places, ocelots have a lot of neighbors. In Peru and in Venezuela, scientists found about 100 to 200 adults per 100 square miles (40 to 80 adult ocelots per 100 square kilometers).

Whose coat is it?

In spite of the high population numbers in some areas, ocelots are a rare and endangered species. They suffered greatly from the demand for their beautiful fur until the 1975 Convention on International Trade in Endangered Species (CITES) made trading their skins illegal. Ocelots do raid people's chicken coops, and many are shot every year for reasons like this.

Ocelots also seem to be unable to survive without the cover provided by forests and thick vegetation. So with increasing destruction of forests and clearing of scrublands for human activities, the ocelot is losing its habitat in much of Central and South America.

◀ *The ocelot lives in forested or scrubby habitats with thick cover. It sometimes hunts in more open areas at night but needs cover to survive.*

South America's small cats

In addition to the ocelot, seven small cats live in diverse habitats in Central and South America: margay, oncilla, Geoffroy's cat, pampas cat, Andean mountain cat and kodkod (see pages 50–51), and jaguarundi. All but the odd-looking jaguarundi (described on pages 48–49) are more closely related to the ocelot than to other small cats.

Small, smaller, smallest

Ocelots, margays, and oncillas are very similar in appearance, but form a series of small, smaller, smallest. The margay weighs between 5½ and 9 pounds (2.5 to 4 kilograms) and has a much longer tail than the other two species. The long tail is adapted to the arboreal (tree-dwelling) habits of this cat, for it spends more time in the trees than most other cats. It hunts at night, in trees, for birds and rodents.

Margays always live in forested habitats, usually humid tropical forests. Although few in numbers, they are widely distributed in

Out on a limb

The margay is the best acrobat of the cat world, with a long tail for balance, broad feet, and very flexible ankle joints that turn through a full half-circle. This flexibility allows the margay to climb easily through trees. Unlike other cats, the margay can dash down a tree trunk like a squirrel to catch prey.

Frank W. Lane/Frank Lane Picture Agency

▶ The beautiful fur of the Geoffroy's cat varies in color from brilliant ocher to silvery gray. All-black Geoffroy's cats have also been seen.

▼ A margay meets a tamandua, a small tree-dwelling anteater of Central and South America.

Warren Garst/Tom Stack & Associates

the forests from Mexico to South America east of the Andes and north of Argentina.

The oncilla, also known as the tiger cat or the little spotted cat, is one of the world's smallest cats. It weighs only 4 to 6 pounds (2 to 3 kilograms), and the head and body length is less than 22 inches (55 centimeters). Its tail is shorter than the margay's, indicating that it spends less time in trees, but it is an agile climber and leaper. The oncilla hunts at night, mainly on the ground, and probably eats birds and rodents.

Strictly a forest cat, the oncilla lives in forests bathed in clouds and humid lowland forests from Costa Rica to northern Argentina. It is rare and the replacement of high-altitude rain forest with coffee plantations may threaten its survival.

Cool cats

Geoffroy's cat, the pampas cat, and the rare kodkod and Andean mountain cat are found in the cooler areas of South America.

Geoffroy's cat is a small, slight cat. At $4\frac{1}{2}$ to 13 pounds (2 to 6 kilograms), it is about the size of a domestic cat. It lives in a variety of habitats, including woodlands, open bushland, rocky areas, and forests along rivers. It hunts at night, both on the ground and in trees, feeding mainly on small mammals such as rodents and on birds.

Geoffroy's cat has the social life of a typical wilderness cat. The adults avoid coming into contact with each other, except when a male and female come together to mate. Adult females live on home ranges that are smaller than male home ranges and often overlap.

The pampas cat lives in open grasslands in Argentina, in high-altitude rain forests in Chile, and at high elevations in the Andes. The size of a sturdy domestic cat, it probably hunts at night for ground-nesting birds and rodents such as guinea pigs.

▲ With a broad face and pointed ears, the pampas cat resembles African wildcats, but they are not closely related. The pampas cat has long manelike hairs on its back that stand erect when it is frightened.

41

Wildcats

Wildcats weigh between 6½ and 17½ pounds (3 to 8 kilograms) and are generally larger and stockier than domestic cats. Otherwise they look quite similar to a tabby cat. Domestic cats and wildcats also seem to interbreed quite freely where the two occur together.

One species

Wildcats are found in many different places in Europe, Africa, the Middle East, and Asia as far as Pakistan and northeastern India. Across this vast area, they are remarkably varied in coat color and markings and in fur length. Based on these differences, dozens of species and subspecies of wildcats were "discovered" over the years. Now, most scientists agree that the wildcats, despite their geographical variety, all belong to a single species, *Felis silvestris*. But they divide the wildcats into three distinct subspecies. The domestic cat is another subspecies of *Felis silvestris*.

European wildcat

The European wildcat lives in forests, where it feeds largely on rats and mice, supplemented with hares, rabbits, and birds. Wildcats used to be hunted down in many parts of Europe, especially in Great Britain, Germany, and Switzerland. In Great Britain, they were considered vermin—vicious predators that took poultry and young sheep and goats. By about 1900, wildcats were extinct in England and very rare in Scotland. During World War I, however, wildcats started to make a comeback when the gamekeepers (who had been their greatest enemies) were off fighting a different foe. Today in Scotland, wildcat numbers have revived and they live wherever the forest habitat is available.

Gunter Ziesler/Bruce Coleman Ltd

◄ *Wildcats hunt on the ground but readily climb trees to escape pursuit. Besides people, the major predators of wildcats are probably larger cats, such as the Eurasian lynx.*

Simon Trevor/Bruce Coleman Ltd

Did you know?

Wildcats are not considered endangered, although they are vulnerable to the effects of habitat loss. The comeback of wildcats in Scotland shows that these versatile small predators can thrive as long as they are not persecuted by people and sufficient habitat remains to support their shy life-style.

Des & Jen Bartlett/Survival Anglia

◄ *An African wildcat in Namibia. All wildcats feed mainly on rodents such as rats and mice, but they supplement their diet with birds, rabbits and hares, and even lizards and large insects.*

African wildcat

The African wildcat is at home in diverse habitats, from open rocky ground to scrubby bush and agricultural croplands. Only Africa's waterless deserts and deepest rain forests don't have any wildcats. This subspecies is believed to be the ancestor of the domestic cat and, unlike the shy European wildcat, is often found living close to villages and farms. Villagers frequently catch and tame young wildcats, which then serve as rat and mouse catchers. In fact, most of the wildcat's natural diet is rodents such as rats and mice.

Indian desert wildcat

The Indian desert wildcat, or steppe wildcat, is adapted to the semi-deserts and steppes of Central Asia, Afghanistan, Pakistan, and northeastern India. It too is a rodent catcher, but its diet also includes gerbils, hares, doves, partridges, peacocks, and sparrows. The desert wildcat is the least known of the three subspecies but is believed to be the ancestor of Asian breeds of domestic cats.

Reproductive behavior

Like so many other species of cats, wildcats are extremely difficult to study in the wild. With their secretive habits and nocturnal hunting behavior, they are rarely seen, even when they live near people. The adults are solitary, living on home ranges which they defend from intruders of the same sex. A female ready to breed, however, may attract several males. The males may sit for hours around a female, howling and trying to approach the female, and fighting with each other, until the female finally chooses her mate.

Two to three young are born after a gestation period of about 65 days, usually in a den in a tree hollow, rock cave, or a hole abandoned by another animal. The kittens are nourished by their mother's milk for about one month and begin to hunt with their mother at about three months of age. By six months of age, the young are independent and the family breaks up.

▼ *A wildcat in South Africa. Depending on where they live, wildcats vary in color, size, and skin patterns.*

Going wild

Feral cats are free-ranging domestic cats. They are cats that have more or less returned to a wild state and do not depend on human caretakers—although for food they may rely on people's garbage and the rats it attracts. Feral cats live in wilderness areas, on uninhabited islands, and even in crowded cities.

Social groups or solitary

While virtually all other cats except lions and cheetahs are solitary animals, feral cats have a surprising variety of social organizations. In some situations they adopt the solitary life-style of their wildcat cousins. But in other cases they live in well-organized social groups, which are somewhat similar to the social groups of lions!

Scientists think that feral cats remain solitary when food is widely dispersed and unpredictable, as the prey of most cats typically is. But if food is abundant and can be found in predictable "patches" such as a farm or a garbage dump, feral cats live in groups to take advantage of it.

Tolerance for group living may be an effect of domestication. In a study in Saudi Arabia, scientists found that wildcats remained solitary although feral cats living in the same area formed groups around a garbage dump.

The same scientists did another study of group-living cats—on several farms in England—and this is what they found: the core members of a group are related females, with a farmyard as their focal point. Beyond the farm outbuildings, each female hunts alone (or with her young) over an area that can be as large as 50 acres (20 hectares); she tends to ignore any other cat hunting nearby, if their ranges overlap. Meanwhile, the males each have a larger area they travel over (as much as 200 acres, or 80 hectares), and they sometimes visit females on other farms.

At the core of any feral cat colony are a group of female cats that are related to each other. A large colony may contain several groups whose members interact more with each other than with the other cats in the colony. But all members of the colony get along. Outsiders are treated with hostility. Females usually keep other females out; males defend against any male intruders.

Within groups, individual cats seem to form "friendships" based on age, social status, sex, and blood ties. For example, they choose to sit together. One behavior, called "rubbing," seems to indicate status in the social-dominance order: the cat that rubs its lips, cheeks, and forehead against another's face is usually subordinate to the cat that's receiving the rubbing.

Male and female feral cats do not form long-term pair bonds, and males take no part in raising kittens. Their social arrangements when mating are not always the same. Sometimes an adult male will stay with a female while she is in estrus (sexually receptive), and this might be from one to four days. But if he is a "roamer," the male will stay with her for just a few hours, then move on in search of another breeding female. An individual male may show both types of behavior within the breeding season, or change between one breeding season and the next!

Females, too, have variable patterns of mothering behavior. Some remain solitary and raise their young alone. Others act as female lions do: as many as four mothers may raise their young communally, in a combined litter. Communal mothering may be more common when the females are closely related, as females in lion prides are.

Male feral cats never form the sort of coalition that we see among lions. Scientists speculate that this, too, is related to food resources. Male lions hunt in groups to capture large prey and to defend their kills from scavengers such as hyenas. Feral cats, eating small prey, have no need to cooperate in the hunt for small animals.

▲ *Human garbage attracts rats and mice, and all three attract feral cats. Such a large patch of food may form the center of activity for a group of feral cats.*

Jane Burton & Kim Taylor/Bruce Coleman Ltd.

John Downer/Planet Earth Pictures

Did you know?

In the small fishing village of Ainoshima in Japan, there are more than 5000 cats per square mile (2000 cats per square kilometer)!

Cats wreak island havoc!

Because they travel with people, domestic cats have reached every corner of the globe. And even with domestication, cats have lost none of their predatory instincts. In many places, especially isolated islands, feral cats found that the local birds and reptiles were easy pickings because they had no experience and thus no fear of predators.

In one amazing case, an entire species—an almost-flightless wren—was wiped out by a single cat! In 1894 a lighthouse keeper arrived with his pet cat on tiny Stephen Island, located in New Zealand's Cook Strait. Within a few months the cat had killed all the Stephen Island wrens. This is an extreme example, but on islands throughout the world, feral cats have had devastating effects on species that aren't used to predators.

Karen Tweedy Holmes/Animals Animals

▲ A group of feral cats is made up of related females that live on overlapping ranges, and males that visit at different times. Each male's range probably includes those of several groups of females.

Cats on the edge

Unlike wildcats, which survive in a wide variety of habitats, some of their relatives have found a niche in extreme habitats.

Adapted to the desert

The sand cat is a desert specialist. This small short-legged cat, weighing only 4½ to 6½ pounds (2 to 3 kilograms), travels the forbidding deserts of North Africa and the Middle East. It lives in a harsh habitat of rolling sand dunes, flat stony plains, and rocky desert. Daytime temperatures may soar to well over 104°F (40°C). At night the temperature plummets below freezing. Water is scarce or nonexistent.

To cope with the desert's extremes of temperature, the sand cat surprisingly has a fine woolly coat. This probably keeps the cat warm while hunting at night—the sand cat is totally nocturnal. But what of the hot days? The cat spends the day in a state of torpor, in which it doesn't move and is oblivious to disturbance. Sometimes it will dig into an underground den in the sand and "switch off." Or it will merely stretch out flat in a hollow or depression in the sand. Its coat matches the sand, so it is very difficult to see.

Coming alive at night, the sand cat hunts for other nocturnal desert-dwellers. In Arabia, these are mostly gerbils, small members of the rodent family. Gerbils get all of their water from dew and moisture in the vegetation they eat; and sand cats get theirs from gerbils! The tiny amount of water available to these animals is one reason for their daytime torpor—any movement during the heat of the day would waste precious water. Other adaptations for desert life include the sand cat's thickly padded and furred paws, which insulate the feet and keep them from slipping in the shifting sand.

Almost the smallest

The black-footed cat is sometimes referred to as the sand cat of southern Africa. Rivaling the rusty-spotted cat for the title of smallest cat in the world, the black-footed cat is confined to arid parts of Botswana, Namibia, and South Africa.

It spends the day under cover, using abandoned aardvark or springhare burrows or termite-mound holes as dens. From the latter, the black-footed cat is often called the ant-hill cat. It eats mice, gerbils, spiders, and insects and may sometimes dig small mammals out of shallow burrows. Like the sand cat, the black-footed cat gets most of its water from its prey.

Like most cats, black-footed cats are solitary, but experienced observers of cats in

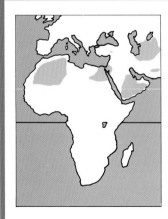

The sand cat

The sand cat is well named. Their habitat once stretched as far east as Pakistan but they now live only in the dry and inhospitable regions of North Africa and the Middle East.

► *The jungle cat's plain, unspotted coat varies in color from sandy or yellow-gray to gray-brown and tawny red. It may even have an all-black coat. The tufted ears led many people to think that the jungle cat was closely related to lynxes, but now everyone agrees that it is not.*

Jean-Paul Ferrero/AUSCAPE

► *The black-footed cat gets its name from the black pads and underparts of its feet. To avoid confusion with the African wildcat, some writers prefer to use a different name for the black-footed cat—the "small spotted cat."*

captivity say that these ones are especially unsocial. They also have a reputation for ferocity—so much so, that in spite of their tiny size they have been reported to attack sheep and even giraffes! These reports, however, have never been confirmed.

If you've seen kittens of a domestic cat, you may have noticed how they rush back to the shelter of their nest when disturbed. But kittens of the black-footed cat (observed in zoos) instead scatter, running away from their mother and each other to find cover wherever they can. Then they "freeze" until their mother gives an all-clear signal— an unusual staccato call, along with an up-and-down move-ment of her ears.

Adapted to wetlands

In contrast to the desert-dwellers, the jungle cat prefers wetlands. It lives not only in the forests of Southeast Asia and India but also in Central Asia and the Middle East.

With long legs and a short tail, jungle cats are the largest members of the domestic cat lineage (see page 67). Their size varies from 35 pounds (16 kilograms) in Central Asia, to 9 to 17$\frac{1}{2}$ pounds (4 to 8 kilograms) in India and Thailand.

Because they hunt on the ground in tall grasses, these cats need very good hearing to find their prey. They eat birds, rodents, small hares, and reptiles, but some may also take larger prey such as porcupines and chital (spotted deer) fawns. Jungle cats are capable of bursts of high speed, running as fast as 20 miles (32 kilometers) per hour, and also make high leaps to pluck birds out of the air.

47

Strange-looking, but truly cats

A few species of cats are remarkable for their unusual, almost uncat-like, appearance. But they are cats, and they behave like cats.

Jaguarundi

With its very long body, a low-slung build, short legs, and a long tail, the jaguarundi looks more like a weasel than a cat. In fact, in Germany this cat is called *Wiezelkatze* (weasel cat), and in parts of Mexico it is commonly known as the "otter cat."

Weighing between 6^{1}/$_{2}$ and 13 pounds (3 to 6 kilograms), jaguarundis feed on whatever is abundant and easy to catch. They hunt on the ground for small mammals, large insects, birds, rabbits, opossums, armadillos, and even small monkeys. Unusual among cats, jaguarundis include fruit in their diet. Also unusual is the fact that they hunt mainly during the day—making them the only small cat you are likely to see in the wild. Despite this, scientists have not yet made a detailed study of their life.

Jaguarundis are found in the southern parts of Arizona, New Mexico, and Texas in the United States, through Mexico and Central America, and into South America as far as northern Argentina. Unlike other cats in this part of the world, the jaguarundi lives in relatively open habitats, as well as in vegetated habitats, including dense forests, dry thorn thickets, and swampy grasslands. Jaguarundis are rarely hunted for their fur, which is unspotted, but they are threatened by the destruction of their habitat. Only a few of these cats still survive in the southwest of the United States, where so much land has been taken over by housing developments. On the other hand, in the 1940s people released jaguarundis (which they had probably kept as pets) into Florida, and a small wild population is now well established there.

Scientists believe that the jaguarundi is related more closely to the big cats than to the other small cats that live in Central and South America.

Flat-headed cat

The flat-headed cat, which has been described as the oddest cat in the world,

▲ *The jaguarundi is one of the most unusual cats. It is often compared to a weasel or an otter.*

◀ *Despite an unusual appearance and small size, the flat-headed cat is actually related to the big cats, along with the fishing cat and the jaguarundi.*

also looks a bit like a weasel. Weighing about 4 1/2 pounds (2 kilograms), it has a long body, short legs, and a short tail. Its head is strangely flattened on top, and it has a long muzzle for a cat. The ears are quite small and set low on the sides of the face.

Native to Thailand, Malaya, Sumatra, and Borneo, flat-headed cats live in tropical forests close to water. Like the fishing cats, they hunt fish and frogs along riverbanks, and probably also eat rodents and birds. And like the fishing cat, the flat-headed cat's claws can be seen even when they are fully retracted. Perhaps because of their similar diet and similar adaptations, flat-headed cats and fishing cats are not found in the same parts of Southeast Asia.

Pallas' cat

Some scientists think that Pallas' cat is closely related to the wildcat, and that its strange features are adaptations to its rugged Central Asian habitat. It lives in deserts, steppes, and the rocky slopes of mountains (up to an altitude of 12 000 feet, about 4000 meters), from the Caspian Sea to southeastern Siberia and China.

About the size of a domestic cat, Pallas' cat is stocky and compact, with short thick legs and a wide head. It appears much larger than it really is because of its very long, thick, fluffy fur, which insulates the cat against the cold temperatures of snowy winters.

Pallas' cats hunt small mammals, such as marmots, pikas, ground squirrels, and hares, and birds, probably at night. During the day they use caves, cracks in rocks, and the burrows of other animals to rest in hiding in their barren habitat. The lack of bushes or trees that could hide the cat may explain why it has short ears, which are set very low on the side of its face. The cat can peer over rocks, looking for prey, while exposing very little of its head.

Pallas' cats have a reputation for remaining wild in captivity. Judging by their facial expression, they seem to be in a permanent state of irritation. In one zoo with lots of small cats, the zoo keeper had a lure that all the other cats seemed to enjoy playing with. When she offered the lure to the Pallas' cat, it ignored it and just stared with a sneer at the keeper. Sneering (quivering the lips over the canine teeth) is a threat expression, which is unique to the Pallas' cat.

▼ *The pupils of the jaguarundi's eyes are round, while most other cats have oval or slitlike pupils. Oval pupils allow for the greater changes in size that are necessary for cats to see well in daylight and in the dark. The jaguarundi's round pupils may be related to its habit of hunting during the day rather than at night.*

Keith and Liz Laidler/Ardea London

Birth spots

Young jaguarundis are born with spotted coats, but the markings disappear as they get older. Other cats that are plain as adults, such as lions and pumas, are also spotted as babies.

Jill D. Mellen

▲ *Pallas' cats have a remarkable ability to climb steep cliffs, moving fluidly up and down the difficult terrain of Central Asia.*

Rare small cats

Borneo's mysterious bay cat

In 1874 a scientist collected and described a single dead specimen of the bay cat from the island of Borneo, in Southeast Asia. About six skins of this species are now in museums around the world. And that's it! There are no descriptions of living bay cats; no scientist has ever seen one. However, bay cats are believed to live in Borneo's dense jungles and in rocky limestone areas at the edges of the jungle. Based on the measurements of the museum skins, the bay cat is about the size of a domestic cat. Its coat is chestnut colored with very light spots, so this species is sometimes called the Bornean red cat.

Shy Andean mountain cats

The Andean mountain cat wins second prize in the "least-known cat" competition. The species' existence in a small area of the high Andes in Peru, Bolivia, Chile, and Argentina was known for more than 100 years only because dead specimens had been taken to museums. Then finally, in 1980, two Argentine scientists saw one and followed it for a couple of hours. They watched the silver gray cat drink from a stream, stroll along a path, and rest for a few minutes. This is all that's known about the mountain cat's behavior, but scientists guess that it lives alone and probably eats small mammals, lizards, and birds.

The Andean mountain cat weighs about 9 pounds (4 kilograms) and is about the size of a large domestic cat. It lives in rocky, treeless areas high in the Andes Mountains. This habitat is windy, dry, and very cold.

Kodkod

The kodkod is another very rare South American cat. It lives in a very small area of Chile and Argentina in evergreen forests and other habitats with trees. People are rapidly destroying these habitats in the kodkod's range, so the species is threatened with extinction.

Kodkods weigh just over 4½ pounds (2 kilograms) and measure 15 to 20 inches (39 to 51 centimeters) in head and body length; the tail is 7½ to 10 inches (19 to 25 centimeters) long. The kodkod's fur is beige or gray-brown with small black spots, but all-black kodkods are also common. Scientists guess that, like other small cats, the adult kodkods live alone and hunt small mammals and birds.

Chinese desert cat

This rare cat does not live in the desert as its name suggests. It inhabits steppes and forests and brush-covered mountains in a very small area of China—Sichuan province, and northward. People hunt the Chinese desert cat for its fur, which is yellowish gray with faint brownish markings. The cat's ears are tipped with a short tuft of fur, and hairy tufts grow between the pads on the bottom of its feet. No one has reported weighing a Chinese desert cat, but their head and body length is 27 to 33 inches (68 to 84 centimeters), making them larger than domestic cats. Nothing else is known about them.

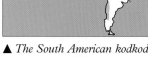

▲ *The South American kodkod.*

◄ *The bay cat from Borneo.*

A new cat

Just 25 years ago, a writer and naturalist named Yukio Togawa heard rumors of a new kind of cat living on the tiny Japanese island of Iriomote. He set off to investigate and learned that the residents of the island knew all about this cat. In fact, they sometimes caught them in traps set for wild boars and greatly enjoyed the unplanned meal they provided. Mr. Togawa took some skins and skulls of cats back to scientists in Japan. Two years later, they officially declared it a new species—the Iriomote cat.

Since then, scientists have learned quite a bit about the new species. Male Iriomote cats weigh about 9 pounds (4 kilograms), and females about 7 pounds (3.25 kilograms). Each adult cat lives alone, traveling over a home range about 1 square mile (2 to 3 square kilometers) in size. Pairs of males and females come together to breed during the winter. The female finds a den in a hollow tree or some other private spot and gives birth to one to four kittens in April or May.

Iriomote cats hunt on land, in trees, and even water. Their diet includes rats, flying foxes (large bats), birds, skinks (small lizards), and insects. They usually hunt at dusk and through the night.

About a third of Iriomote Island is now a protected reserve, and the Japanese have declared the Iriomote cat a national treasure. Even so, the number of cats seems to be falling. Between 50 and 100 Iriomote cats share their small island, which is only 112 square miles (290 square kilometers), with a growing population of people who farm sugarcane, rice, and pineapples. The cats' habitat is being destroyed for farms, roads, and dams. In addition, some cats are still accidentally killed in boar traps, and feral cats, which are not native to the island, may compete with the Iriomote cats for the same prey.

▼ *The Iriomote cat is one of the rarest and most threatened small cats in the world.*

Tadaaki Imaizumi/Nature Production

The domestication of cats

Cats were first domesticated at least 4000 years ago in ancient Egypt, and perhaps even earlier than this. The jawbone of a cat from about 6000 B.C. was found in one of the first human settlements in Cyprus, an island where no wildcats occur. So even 8000 years ago, people might have been carrying tamed cats with them when they moved to a new area.

Wildcat ancestors

Why and how did people domesticate cats? The ancestors of domestic cats were wildcats of the North African subspecies (see pages 42–43). Some think that these cats were naturally attracted to the rats and mice that always exist around villages and farms. The people tolerated and even cared for the cats that helped rid them of these unwanted rodents. Eventually, the cats came to depend on people for food and shelter, and they became domesticated.

Other scientists point out that wildcats today go out of their way to avoid people, so they doubt this story. Instead, they believe that people first captured wildcat kittens, and tamed them for pets. It is a common human habit, found among people all over the world, to keep tamed wild animals for pets. Many types of animals may have first been domesticated after a history of being captured as pets.

However cats became domesticated, they were common household animals in Egypt by 1500 B.C. Cats also came to be seen as sacred and were worshipped as representing various Egyptian gods and goddesses (see page 64). But cats were slow to spread to Europe because Egyptians were forbidden to export them. Even in Roman times, domestic cats were considered quite unusual, and it wasn't until the 1800s that cats started to become the very popular pets they are to Western people today.

▲ A cat mummy. Cat owners in ancient Egypt lavished attention on their cats in life and death. After their death, cats were often mummified and buried.

▼ Three birds seem to have been caught by a cat in this painting from an ancient Egyptian tomb. Cats first appeared in Egyptian art in about 2000 B.C.

Movers and shakers

For at least the past 2000 years, domestic cats have followed people to the far corners of the Earth. Some cats have been shipboard stowaways; others moved with their owners in high style. But wherever people went, so did cats. Today, the descendants of those cats often reflect the national origins of the people they accompanied.

Most of the New England area of the United States was settled by British colonists, and the modern cats of New England are still very similar to English cats. But the cats of New York (which was first settled by the Dutch) are today closer to the Dutch cats in the Netherlands than they are to most of the New England cats.

What's the difference?

▶ *A feral cat makes its home in the hollow of a river red gum in Central Australia. Feral cats are a threat to Australia's small native marsupials.*

Domestication has created fewer changes in cats than it has in some other domestic animals. And wherever domestic cats live unconfined and in the same range as wildcats (many parts of Europe, Asia, and Africa), some interbreeding between wildcats and domestic cats takes place. But in general, domestic cats are smaller than their wild cousins, and have smaller brains.

▲ *Wildcats are solitary animals, larger and more aggressive than domestic cats.*

Domestic cats are more docile than wildcats. Two factors account for this. First, adult domestic cats look and act more like kittens than adult wildcats. Second, domestic cats have relatively smaller adrenal glands than wildcats. These glands produce the chemicals that make an animal, including you, scared, run away, or fight back when some danger threatens. With smaller adrenal glands producing fewer chemicals, a domestic cat is far calmer than a wild one.

Today's pet cats

About 30 different breeds of domestic cats have found favor with pet owners around the world. But unlike dogs, which people have bred into a vast array of sizes, shapes, and habits, cat breeds differ mainly in the color and quality of their fur.

Cat fanciers divide cat breeds into two broad groups. British breeds (which may be European or American) are usually stocky and have heavy coats. Foreign breeds, such as the Siamese, are slimmer and have shorter hair than British breeds. Cat breeds are also divided into long-haired, such as Persians, and short-haired, which is the natural type.

For most of the thousands of years that cats have been domesticated, people took little control over their breeding. But gradually, differences developed between domestic cats in different parts of the world. The cats adapted to local conditions such as climate, which affected their fur and build. For instance, the slim, short-haired Siamese, Burmese, Birman, and Korat were adapted to the hot climates of Southeast Asia, while the heavier British breeds were adapted to the colder climates of northern Europe. Long-haired varieties, such as Persian and Angora, came from parts of the Middle East and Central Asia.

Many of the other modern breeds, however, were created by Western cat fanciers during the past 120 years. These breeders were interested in unusual or abnormal features that seemed to appeal to people. This process continues today, producing unnatural breeds such as the nearly hairless Sphinx, a cat that could never survive in the wild.

What color will your cat be?

The fur of domestic cats comes in different colors from all black to all white and in many patterns from plain to spotted and striped. Scientists have learned that all of this variety comes from about nine pairs of genes or alleles. These alleles carry the "instructions" for every cat's color and pattern. The combination of alleles any particular cat inherits from its parents determines what color and pattern will appear in its fur.

The wild-type coloration is called the striped or mackeral tabby. This is the pattern of the wildcat ancestor of domestic cats. The genetic instructions for this pattern are on the tabby allele, symbolized by the capital letter T. Another mutant allele, called t^b, gives instructions for a blotched tabby, but T is dominant to it. This means that if t^b is paired with T, t^b's instructions will not be carried out; t^b is called a recessive gene. Alleles come in pairs, so if a cat inherits either two tabby alleles, TT, or one tabby and one blotched, Tt^b, the cat will be a typical tabby. But if the cat inherits two blotched alleles, $t^b t^b$, it will

be blotched. Each parent donates one allele to its young, so a cat will always be blotched if both parents are $t^b t^b$, or, about one-quarter of the time, when both parents have mixed Tt^b alleles.

But this just gets us tabby and blotched fur. What about all the other colors and patterns? Other alleles give instructions that can mask or change the basic tabby fur. The basic tabby has an agouti allele, A, which gives instructions for the background coloration. But a mutant allele, a or non-agouti, makes the background black so stripes and blotches cannot be seen. Again, the agouti or A allele is dominant, but if a cat inherits two a alleles it will be black.

So what color will your cat be? It's hard to say. Unless you know a lot about the parents' ancestors, you can never be sure when some recessive alleles might match up and produce some surprising kittens.

▲ Cat breeds are divided into short-haired and long-haired. Persian longhairs (such as the one pictured above) and Angoras originally came from parts of the Middle East and Central Asia.

◄ This short-haired tabby cat with its stocky body is a typical British domestic cat breed. It is very similar in appearance to its wildcat ancestors.

► A well-groomed pet Persian cat.

▼ The instructions for different coat colors and patterns in domestic cats are carried on about nine pairs of genes or alleles. Common cat coat colors are shown below, from left to right: striped or mackerel tabby; Burmese; tortoiseshell and white female; dominant white; ginger or sex-linked orange female; gray (or blue) dilution; blotched tabby and white; non-agouti black.

James Serpell

The conservation of small cats

With just a few exceptions, small cats face an uncertain future in the wild. And uncertain is the key word. For many species of small cats, we simply don't know what their status is.

Threats to their survival

The lack of information raises a thorny issue in conservation: should we assume a little-known species is doing fine unless good evidence shows that it is not? Or should we assume it is doing poorly, given that so many species, from cats to bats and birds and frogs, are declining around the world?

The bay cat is a good example. It is not on the United States Endangered Species List, and on the World Conservation Union's (IUCN) list it is detailed as "rare." Rare, indeed. No scientist has ever seen one, far less been able to count them to determine their status. It seems likely that logging and clearing of forests for agriculture in the bay cat's habitat in Borneo might have had some impact on bay cats, but how would we know? The same uncertainty clouds the status of Chinese desert cats, Pallas' cats, and kodkods. At the moment, there are no programs or people in place to monitor the status of small cats that are listed as rare or endangered.

It is easy, however, to list the factors that threaten the survival of many species of small cats:

1. Uncontrolled hunting for sport and fur This threatens most of the small, spotted cat species as well as sand cats.

2. Destruction of tropical rain forests Loss of rain forest threatens clouded leopards, marbled cats, African and Asian golden cats, ocelots, jaguarundis, margays, oncillas, and Iriomote cats.

3. Conversion of tropical grasslands and dry forest to agriculture Cats such as pampas cats, jaguarundis, Geoffroy's cats, and black-footed cats are likely to be affected.

4. Expansion of pasture lands into dry and mountainous habitats As human populations increase, traditional herders of livestock are moving into once-remote habitats. This brings people into contact—and conflict—with species like Pallas' cats, Chinese desert cats, sand cats, kodkods, and Andean mountain cats.

5. Loss of riverside habitats Fishing cats and flat-headed cats, which depend on water, suffer when human activities take over or pollute river habitats.

6. Fragmentation and isolation of habitats Even when habitats are not entirely destroyed, human activities increasingly break habitats into patches. The patches become "islands" surrounded by roads, villages, farms, and factories, which often prevent animals from leaving their patch and keep others from entering it. This leads to inbreeding among the cats and, eventually, to the loss of the genetic diversity needed for the species' long-term survival. For most species, inbreeding and loss of genetic diversity leads to reduced reproduction, high infant mortality (death of kittens), and increased susceptibility to disease.

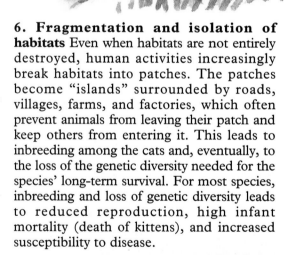

▲ *With 100 or fewer Iriomote cats sharing only one small island, this species is likely to suffer from inbreeding and loss of genetic diversity. This species is also threatened by habitat destruction and competition with feral cats.*

◀ *Kodkods are not listed as endangered but too little is known about them to say they are not. Kodkods are protected by law from hunting in their native Chile and Argentina, but they are probably declining due to habitat loss.*

Eduardo J. Ramilo/Focus

► *Four subspecies of the wide-ranging jaguarundi are endangered. Although rarely hunted for their fur, many jaguarundis are shot while raiding poultry yards, and habitat destruction is taking its toll on this adaptable predator.*

Francois Gohier/AUSCAPE

► *Asian golden cat.*

In time, extinction of the population results. Scientists estimate that at least 250 breeding individuals within an area are necessary to prevent loss of genetic diversity and, ultimately, extinction. The Spanish lynx, now found only in a few isolated patches, and true island species such as the Iriomote cat, are in the greatest danger of extinction due to inbreeding.

Virtually all small cats are threatened by habitat loss and fragmentation. The species that are likely to fare best in the future are those that are not overly disturbed by human activities. Some species can even take advantage of the presence of humans. Servals, for instance, thrive on the increased rodent population that always comes with human agricultural activities. But close contact with people is risky. Poultry and livestock are also attractive prey to most small cats, and people object to losing their farm animals—their food and income—to cats. As a result, they usually try to kill the cats.

The future of small cats in the wild will depend on us learning how to accommodate the needs of people and the needs of cats so we can both live without conflict. The challenge in most cases is to find out precisely what the needs of these cats are.

The skin trade

For a long time, people all over the world have prized garments made of the beautiful fur of cats. In many cultures, possession of cat skins is a symbol of high status. In other places, capes and coats made of cat fur are worn in religious rites and cultural ceremonies. In the late 1800s, international trade in cat skins began to boom when a large market developed among Westerners for coats made of cat fur.

Big business

Most of this skin trade was in the fur of large striped and spotted cats—tigers, leopards, snow leopards, cheetahs, and jaguars. Clouded leopards and lynxes were also sought after. By the early 1960s, this trade was a major threat to the survival of these species and all were becoming increasingly rare. In the 1960s and 1970s, many countries passed laws to protect their big cats from further hunting or trapping, and in the late 1960s, many fur traders agreed to stop trading in big cat furs. Finally in 1975, many countries began to follow the

It takes up to 40 dumb animals to make a fur coat.

But only one to wear it.

LYNX
Fighting the fur trade
P.O. Box 509 Dunmow, Essex Tel 0371 2016

If you don't want animals gassed, electrocuted, trapped or strangled, don't buy a fur coat.

Fur in the marketplace

Fur coats are becoming less and less popular in the West, but hundreds of thousands of small cats are still hunted or trapped each year for the fur trade. The advertisement above was designed to make rich Westerners think carefully about the effects of fashion on cats.

In poorer countries, ocelots are still hunted and killed for their pelts. Even though ocelots are an endangered species, and international trade in them is banned, many people find that the rewards of selling illegally caught skins outweigh the risks of being caught and punished. The ocelot pelts on the left are openly displayed for sale in a market in Ecuador.

▲ *A lynx on the prowl. Small cats such as these are now threatened because many countries have now passed laws to protect their big cats.*

cats for fur. North American lynxes, bobcats, margays, and ocelots were particularly hard hit. By 1988, margays, ocelots, and oncillas were so reduced in numbers that they were moved from Appendix II to Appendix I. In the 1980s the fur traders turned to still other small cats.

Geoffroy's cats are now the hardest hit of all the small cats, followed by jungle cats, wildcats, and leopard cats. The skins of almost half a million Geoffroy's cats were exported from Argentina alone between 1976 and 1980. China harvests about 100 000 leopard cat skins each year. Bobcats and North American lynxes also continue to be harvested at a rate of about 70 000 bobcat skins and 18 000 to 20 000 lynx skins per year.

Part of the reason for these enormous numbers is the simple fact that it takes lots of small cat skins to make a single coat. The average fur coat requires 7.5 North American lynx pelts, 15 leopard cat pelts, 25 Geoffroy's cat pelts, and 30 wildcat pelts! As long as even a small demand exists for cat fur coats, a large number of cats will die to satisfy the demand.

Fairly reliable numbers exist for the legal trade in cat skins. For bobcats and North American lynxes, the annual harvest is closely regulated and populations of both these species are either stable or increasing in numbers. The adaptable leopard cat also seems to be holding its own. But the status of other cats hunted for the fur trade—and virtually all the small cats are traded in at least small numbers—is unknown.

There is also a very large illegal trade in striped and spotted cat skins. Along with habitat destruction, this may be the greatest threat to the survival of endangered cats, big and small.

regulations of the Convention on International Trade in Endangered Species (CITES). Under CITES, commercial trade in big cats and some smaller cats, such as clouded leopards and marbled cats, is banned. These species are known as Appendix I species. All the other cats are Appendix II, which means they can be legally traded if the trade and its effect on the species are closely watched.

Unfortunately, as the big cats became rare and trade slowed down in the 1960s and 1970s, fur traders turned to the small

▶ *The ocelot may possess one of the most beautiful of all spotted fur coats. But the coats belong on ocelots not on people.*

Saving small cats

What's being done to save small cats? Too little. Conservation action is influenced not only by a species' actual need but also by politics and economics as well as the popularity of a species with the public.

▶ *The oncilla is becoming rarer as its habitat is destroyed.*

Protection for big and small cats

"Save the sand cat (or kodkod or margay)" will never evoke the worldwide concern that the slogan "Save the tiger" did in the 1970s. No one will ever be able to argue that a serval or caracal is worth the 151,000 in tourist dollars that a single male lion "earns" each year for Kenya—an important reason for saving lions. But, fortunately, efforts to save the big cats will also help the small ones.

Any national park or protected reserve large enough to sustain jaguars, for instance, is likely also to sustain margays, oncillas, and ocelots. Reserves for tigers in Sumatra could help protect the six species of small cats that live on this huge island. In many parts of the world the best way, perhaps the only way, to save small cats may be to save big ones.

Another key to small cat survival, particularly small, spotted cats, is management and control of hunting for fur. Studies of bobcats and lynxes in North America indicate that these species can survive a certain level of carefully managed "harvesting." Because bobcat and lynx skins earn rural hunters some $15 million per year, it is in their interests to protect the cats so they can earn this income year after year. Unfortunately, most developing countries do not have the resources to manage the harvest of spotted cats, and poaching and smuggling the skins of protected species are widespread.

How technology can help

After years of neglect, research on small cats in the wild is slowly increasing. This is largely due to improved technology, such as the use

▼ *North American lynxes have been a favorite target of skin hunters.*

Alan & Sandy Carey

◀ *The Chinese desert cat is hunted for its thick fur.*

an antenna and radio receiver, the biologist can locate and follow the cat by listening to its radio signal. Information collected by radiotracking over a period of time reveals when the cat is active, how far and where it travels, and the size and boundaries of its home range. Radiotelemetry studies are responsible for most of what is known about bobcats, lynxes, ocelots, and Geoffroy's cats in the wild, but many other species haven't been studied yet.

Some encouragement comes from groups such as the IUCN's Cat Specialist Group. More than 100 of the world's leading cat experts serve on this panel, which prepares conservation action plans and advises governments and other organizations on important cat conservation questions. While many of their efforts concern big cats, this group is beginning to focus more strongly on the needs of small cats.

What you can do

People all over the world must show more concern for small cats. This will happen only when more people learn about the small cats and what threatens them. You can help by sharing what you have learned about kodkods and bay cats, oncillas and marbled cats, and all the rest. It is up to all of us to ensure that small cats don't disappear.

of radiotelemetry, to study these secretive creatures. Without such methods, most small cats are extremely difficult to study. Imagine, for instance, a biologist trying to follow an oncilla as it hunts at night in dense tropical rain forest—provided, that is, the scientist could find one to follow!

With radiotelemetry, a small cat can be captured, outfitted with a collar that gives out a radio signal, then released. Equipped with

Studying cats

Small cats are not easy to study. They are often secretive, solitary animals that live in remote and isolated places far from human settlement. Nevertheless, it is important to learn how and where these animals live, what they eat, and how many there are. Only then can we determine what must be done to save them.

Scientists have developed new ways of studying cats. The Eurasian lynx in the top photo is being fitted with a radio collar so that scientists can follow its movements. Without the technology of radiotelemetry, it is almost impossible to study small cats, which are mostly secretive forest-dwellers that are active at night.

Another useful technique for studying the movements of small cats uses video recordings of images picked up by heat detectors, as shown in the bottom picture. With this technique, scientists can tell whether a cat visits or passes a particular location. It can also reveal whether the cat is alone or with a mate or kittens.

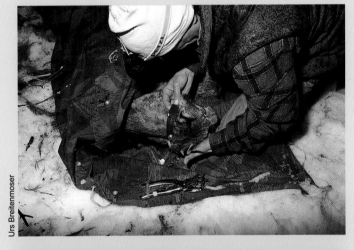

Urs Breitenmoser

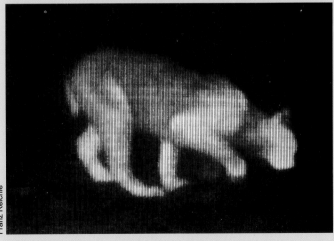

Franz Reichle

61

Small cats in zoos

If you visit your local zoo, you're almost certain to find tigers and lions, and at least one other big cat—perhaps a leopard or a jaguar or a cheetah. But how many small cats can you find?

Why are there so few?

In North America, bobcats and lynxes are fairly common, as are servals and caracals. But few zoos, even the biggest, exhibit more than a few species of small cats. The National Zoological Park in Washington, D.C., for instance, exhibits only bobcats, servals, and Geoffroy's cats.

One reason for this is that unlike their larger relatives, small cats do not breed well in zoos. This has prevented all but a few small cat species, such as bobcats and servals, from becoming widespread in zoos. Another reason is that they are not as popular with the public as big cats. People flock to admire the powerful grace of tigers and the sleek elegance of cheetahs. But small cats resemble everyone's pet tabby and so they have little of the allure of their majestic cousins. Also, small cats do not make lively exhibits—like all cats, they tend to sleep except when they are eating.

Zoo exchange programs

Small cat species that breed well in captivity almost certainly find wide acceptance in zoos. Any single zoo can hold only a limited number of individuals of any particular species. Through formal and informal exchange networks between zoos, extra animals are taken to other zoos, where they breed, and, in turn, their extra animals go to other zoos. If the program is successful, the species will be held in an increasing number of zoos.

▼ Ocelots behave in their zoo enclosure much as they do in the wild. Providing conditions that allow cats to display natural behavior patterns is a goal of modern zoos.

Jill D. Mellen

Small cat crusader

Jill Mellen, who is now a conservation research coordinator at the Washington Park Zoo in Portland, Oregon, has devoted most of her career to small cats.

To learn why small cats breed poorly in zoos, she studied the behavior of males and females in twenty species. Mellen found that healthy cats and those housed as single pairs were most likely to reproduce. The other factor affecting small cat breeding was more surprising. Mellen learned that the more time a keeper spent with the cats, the more likely the cats were to reproduce.

Given the solitary nature of cats, Mellen would have predicted the opposite. After rethinking it, however, it made sense. Keepers are part of any zoo cat's life. They visit daily to clean enclosures and feed their charges. Mellen thinks that the more "comfortable" cats are with their keepers, and with their zoo environment, the more likely they are to breed successfully.

In the past, breeding animals in zoos was of little concern. Not much attention was paid to an animal's basic nutritional or health needs let alone anything more. It was thought that replacement animals could always be collected from the wild. But times—and zoos—have changed.

Surviving in zoos and in the wild

Modern zoos see conservation as their highest priority. Improved diets and health care, and appropriate captive habitats and social groupings, mean that most animals live long, productive lives in zoos. Very few animals are taken from the wild. In North America and elsewhere, zoos are also cooperating in programs to save populations of endangered species. The American Association of Zoological Parks and Aquariums (AAZPA), for instance, coordinates Species Survival Plans (SSPs) for more than 55 endangered species. These plans are designed to ensure that genetically diverse zoo populations survive even though wild populations are declining. The zoo population is a back-up to conservation efforts for animals in the wild.

SSPs exist for most of the endangered big cats—tigers, snow leopards, cheetahs, and Asian lions—but for only one small cat: the clouded leopard. This is mainly because too few individuals of most small cat species exist in zoos. There are just not enough to start an effective breeding program—even if they could be encouraged to breed. And, of course, legally as well as morally, more individuals cannot usually be obtained from the wild. Many small cat species are in danger of going extinct in captivity.

The Pakistani sand cat, for instance, is probably extinct in the wild. Only nine live in zoos, and they are all descendants of a single breeding pair. Due to inbreeding, sand cats are likely to die out in North American zoos, as they already have in European zoos. Pampas cats, Pallas' cats, rusty-spotted cats, and marbled cats face the same fate. Other rare small cats, such as Chinese desert cats, kodkods, and Andean mountain cats, are not known to be in any captive collection. Without a zoo "back-up team," efforts to save small cats in the wild become all the more important.

▼ *A pair of jaguarundis in a naturalistic zoo enclosure. Thanks to improved diets and health care, and more consideration of social and environmental needs, many cats in zoos live longer, healthier lives than do their cousins in the wild. Small cats, however, do not breed well in zoos.*

Cats and culture

Browsing in your local bookstore, you're likely to find a dozen or more books devoted to domestic cats. Some are serious tomes about breeding and showing pedigreed cats. Others, such as *101 Uses for a Dead Cat*, poke fun at our obsession with cats. Cartoonist Jim Davis' Garfield moved from the comic pages to books, calendars, bed sheets, and even credit card commercials. Today, everyone loves cats, except those who utterly despise them! There is really no middle ground.

Small cats in mythology

Among the small cats, domestic cats dominate as cultural icons (or symbols)— not enough is known about other small cats to have captured human imaginations the way tigers, lions, and leopards have. In Norse mythology, lynxes were sacred to Freya, the goddess of love and beauty, and lynxes drew her chariot when she went into battle. Some African peoples held the golden cat in special regard, and its skins formed part of a chief's ceremonial dress. But overall, small cats have been as ignored culturally as they have been scientifically.

Cats on the Nile

Cats were first domesticated in ancient Egypt, and this is where they first appeared in art. By about 1500 B.C., cats played an important role in the complex structure of Egyptian religion. Male cats were sacred to the sun god, Ra, who turned into a tomcat in his daily battles with the serpent of darkness. Female cats represented the mother goddess, Bastet, and later other female deities as well. Cats were also associated with the moon—a source of the Earth's fertility—and the lunar cycle. In modern times, the association of cats with the moon can be seen in *Alice in Wonderland*: the Cheshire cat appears and disappears, like the moon, with a huge crescent-shaped grin.

Egyptian cat cults persisted for about one thousand years, but the rise of Christianity in Europe changed attitudes toward cats. Because they were associated with ancient pagan (or non-Christian) mother goddesses, Europeans of the Middle Ages persecuted cats for hundreds of years. Cats were depicted as agents of the Devil, and the favorites of witches. Cats, especially black ones, came to symbolize bad luck, and became scape-goats for human misfortune. Christian festivals were highlighted by the torture and massacre of cats by the hundreds. In Elizabethan times, cats were caught and stuffed into leather bags, which were hung from trees and used for archery practice. (This may be the origin of the expression "letting the cat out of the bag.") These attitudes slowly began to change in the 1600s and 1700s, but cats did not begin to achieve real popularity again until the middle of the 1800s. And even today, the link between cats and witches, and black cats and bad luck, persists in popular thought.

An ancient cat

This bronze sculpture of the Egyptian cat goddess Bastet dates from around 751 to 656 B.C. The cat once symbolized the feminine virtues of beauty, grace, fertility, and motherhood. In this statue, Bastet is holding her three emblems: The sistrum in her right hand symbolizes the worship of Isis, another goddess to whom cats were sacred; the shield in Bastet's left hand demonstrates her fierceness; and the basket on her arm is where her kittens will be carried.

◄ *The battles between Tom and Jerry have entertained children and adults for many years. Photo:*

▲ *A wildcat devours a partridge in this mosaic from a Naples museum. Wildcats and other small cats only rarely appear in art, but the vast number of representations, in all media, of domestic cats makes up for the absence of the others.*

Poetry in motion

Cats have long inspired artists, who strive to capture on paper or canvas their predatory grace and mysterious aloofness. Cat metaphors and similes abound in literature and everyday speech. Poet Carl Sandburg's image in "Fog" is compelling:

> The fog comes
> on little cat feet.
> It sits looking
> over the harbor and city
> on silent haunches
> and then moves on.

We speak of "raining cats and dogs." We describe the over-satisfied wealthy as "fat cats," and some women we call "catty," with an unmistakable meaning that takes a dozen or more words to express in any other way.

Cats are often the main character in literature. The brilliant British author of comic tales, P. G. Wodehouse begins *The Story of Webster* with the irresistible line "Cats are not dogs!" and proceeds to relate the story of Lancelot, a young man who has taken in his saintly uncle's cat. Webster, a cat with "the exquisite poise which one sees in high dignitaries of the Church," threatens to ruin Lancelot's life by imposing a silent, supercilious disapproval of Lancelot, his fiancee, and their Bohemian ways. Then Webster discovers the pleasures of "Demon Rum," and entirely loses his dignity. For Lancelot, "Webster, that seeming pillar of austere virtue, was one of the boys, after all. Never again would Lancelot quail beneath his eye. He had the goods on him." As writer Henry James said, "Cats and monkeys, monkeys and cats—all human life is there."

▶ *An illustration by Arthur Rackham of "As I was going to St. Ives," which was printed in a 1913 edition of Mother Goose. In the Middle Ages, Europeans associated cats with witches and sorcery, and even today, superstitions about cats being omens of evil and bad luck persist in Western culture.*

Glossary

CANINE TEETH	The teeth between the front incisor teeth and the side molars. Long, sharp canine teeth are a feature of all cats.
CARNIVORA	A large scientific grouping, or order, of mammals, most of which are meat-eaters. Cats belong to the order Carnivora. So do dogs and bears.
CARNIVORE	Any animal that eats meat or flesh. Many animals (including people) are carnivores but do not belong to the order Carnivora.
CONSERVATION	The attempt to maintain the earth's natural resources, including wildlife, for future generations.
DIGITIGRADE STANCE	Walking on the toes, so that the heels do not touch the ground. The foot bones of cats are modified so that only their toes touch the ground. Human stance, walking with the entire foot on the ground, is called plantigrade.
ESTRUS	The period when a female mammal is ready to mate with a male to produce young.
EXTINCT	No longer living. When the last living member of a species dies, the species becomes extinct.
FAMILY	A scientific grouping of several species with similar features. Cats belong to the family Felidae.
GENETIC DIVERSITY	The amount of variation that exists in the genes of all the individual members of a species.
GENUS	A scientific grouping of species that are more closely related to each other than to any other species.
HABITAT	The place where an animal lives in the wild, such as a forest or a grassland. An animal's habitat provides food, water, shelter, and the right environment for the animal's survival.
HOME RANGE	The area that an animal travels over, during the course of a year, to find food and shelter, to find mates, and to raise young.
INBREEDING	Breeding between close relatives. Inbreeding often results in the death of many infants, greater susceptibility to disease, and reproductive problems.
POACHING	Hunting wild animals illegally.
PREDATOR	An animal that hunts, kills, and eats other animals to survive.
PREY	Animals that are hunted, killed, and eaten by other animals called predators.
PRIDE	A group of lions.
PRIMATES	Monkeys, apes, and people.
SCAVENGER	An animal that survives by eating meat killed by other predators.
SPECIES	A group of animals with very similar features. Individual members of a species are able to breed and produce live young that are fertile (able to breed when they themselves

become adults); they do not breed with members of other species. The species is the basic unit in scientific classification of plants and animals.

SUBSPECIES   Members of a species that consistently differ in certain features from other members of the species—although not enough so that individuals can no longer breed and produce live, fertile young. Subspecies are usually separated from each other by barriers such as seas or high mountains.

TERRITORY   An area that an animal (or group of animals) lives in, and which it defends from other members of its species, especially those of the same sex. An animal's home range is called a territory if the animal does not allow others of the same sex to enter it.

List of scientific names

clouded leopard	*Neofelis nebulosa*	Iriomote cat	*Felis iriomotensis*
marbled cat	*Felis marmorata*	jaguarundi	*Felis yagouaroundi*
North American lynx	*Lynx canadensis*	ocelot	*Felis pardalis*
bobcat	*Lynx rufus*	margay	*Felis wiedii*
Eurasian lynx	*Lynx lynx*	oncilla	*Felis tigrina*
Spanish lynx	*Lynx pardinus*	kodkod	*Felis guigna*
caracal	*Lynx caracal*	Geoffroy's cat	*Felis geoffroyi*
serval	*Felis serval*	Andean mountain cat	*Felis jacobita*
African golden cat	*Felis aurata*	pampas cat	*Felis colocolo*
Asian golden cat	*Felis temmincki*	wildcat	*Felis silvestris*
leopard cat	*Felis bengalensis*	Pallas' cat	*Felis manul*
fishing cat	*Felis viverrina*	jungle cat	*Felis chaus*
flat-headed cat	*Felis planiceps*	black-footed cat	*Felis nigripes*
rusty-spotted cat	*Felis rubiginosa*	sand cat	*Felis margarita*
bay cat	*Felis badia*	Chinese desert cat	*Felis bieti*

The name game

The chart above lists the common and scientific names of the small cats covered in this book. As you can see, each scientific name is made up of two words. The first word is the genus (or group) the cat belongs to—most of the small cats are included in the genus *Felis*. The second word is the species name, for example *wiedii*. Together, the genus and species words form a unique combination to identify a unique type of animal, such as *Felis wiedii*, whose common name is margay. The scientific names are usually from Latin or Greek words. This system, called the binomial (two-word) system, was invented by the Swedish naturalist Carolus Linnaeus in 1758.

Why are there special, scientific names for animals? One reason is that this helps eliminate confusion when the same animal is called different names by different people. For instance, the cat we call an oncilla is sometimes called a little tiger cat. In Spanish, both oncillas and ocelots are sometimes called *tigrillo* or *gato tigre*. Unless there was a standard way to refer to these animals, scientists wouldn't know whether a report talked about an oncilla or an ocelot!

Another reason for scientific names is that they say something about how animals are related to each other. If an animal is given a species name that is unique it means that scientists think it is a species separate from all other species. So, for example, scientists who agree that North American lynx and Eurasian lynx are different species give them different names, as we do in this book. Scientists who think they are the same species call them by one name, *Lynx lynx*.

Species that are more closely related to each other than to other kinds of cats are grouped together into a higher category, the genus. Right now, almost all of the small cats, except for the lynxes and the clouded leopards, are "lumped" into the genus *Felis*, and this book follows that practice. But as more is learned about the genetic similarities and differences among the cat lineages, this is likely to change. To give just one example, the marbled cat is probably very closely related to the clouded leopard. In the future, scientists will probably change its genus name to reflect this. So don't be surprised if you find different scientific names for some of these small cats in other books.

Index